MW00328542

Marco Mezzadri

Essential
Italian

An elementary (A1) to upper-intermediate
(B2) **grammar book** for students of Italian
as a foreign language.

With diagnostic test.

Guerra Edizioni

I edizione
© Copyright 2004 Guerra Edizioni - Perugia

Proprietà letteraria riservata

ISBN 88-7715-810-7

3.   2.   1.
2006   2005   2004

Versione inglese di:
Anila Scott-Monkhouse e Patricia Taylor

Disegni: Andrea Bruni

Ha collaborato:
Linuccio Pederzani

La sezione di autovalutazione è tratta dal testo Pederzani L.,
Mezzadri M., *Grammatica essenziale della lingua italiana.
Esercizi supplementari e test*, Guerra Edizioni, Perugia 2001.

Per contattare la casa editrice: geinfo@guerra-edizioni.com
Per contattare l'autore: mezzadri@guerra-edizioni.com

 Questo libro fa parte del progetto *Rete!*

*"**Essential Italian**" with a diagnostic test section*, is an elementary (A1) to upper-intermediate (B2) grammar book for students of Italian as a foreign language. The book follows a progressive grammar syllabus, using graded vocabulary suitable for each stage of development.

There are 96 units and 3 appendixes, as well as a section with a diagnostic test and answer key.

Each unit covers a particular grammar point and the grammar areas are presented in clear and simple language, avoiding many terms no longer relevant to modern day Italian.

"**Essential Italian**" should not be considered a prescriptive or exhaustive grammar book, but as a tool for the practical and immediate use of the language.

The three appendixes have been included to make the text more user-friendly. The first two appendixes deal with problematic areas related to phonetics and written Italian. The third appendix contains brief, simplified explanations regarding the metalanguage used in the theoretical part of the book and can be used as a study aid for the student in an attempt to minimise any problems arising from such specific terminology.

A great effort has been made to greatly reduce the role of specific terminology in the grammar explanations.

In some of the units follow-up references are made to the appendixes; these will hopefully help and stimulate the students to overcome any difficulties that may be linked to the use of specific terminology.

The book also offers a list of units (Contents) and an Index at the end of the book for quick and easy reference.

*"**Essential Italian**"* can be used in class or at home alongside the language textbook as a way of offering immediate practice and consolidation of the structures presented in class or as a tool for extension or revision work on grammar. The book is also suitable for individual work. It can be used as a source of reference for both self-study students and learners on a language course.

In the English edition rather literal translations may be given in order to clearly illustrate the grammar point being explained in the unit.

Contents

Unità	1	The verb *essere* (infinitive - present indicative)	11
Unità	2	The verb *avere* (infinitive - present indicative)	13
Unità	3	Present indicative (1) - (regular verbs)	15
Unità	4	Present indicative (2) - (regular verbs)	17
Unità	5	Forms of the definite article	19
Unità	6	The indefinite article	21
Unità	7	Nouns and gender	23
Unità	8	The plural forms of nouns (1)	25
Unità	9	The plural forms of nouns (1) (irregular plurals)	27
Unità	10	Adjectives	28
Unità	11	Possessive adjectives and pronouns	31
Unità	12	Demonstrative adjectives	33
Unità	13	Demonstrative pronouns	35
Unità	14	*Vorrei* and *potrei (would like and could)*	37
Unità	15	Cardinal numbers	38
Unità	16	Ordinal numbers	40
Unità	17	The time	42
Unità	18	Dates, years and centuries	45
Unità	19	Question words (1)	47
Unità	20	Question words (2) and exclamations	49
Unità	21	Adverbs (1)	51
Unità	22	Adverbs (2)	53
Unità	23	Combined propositions with the definite article	55
Unità	24	Prepositions of place (1)	56
Unità	25	Prepositions and expressions of place (1)	59
Unità	26	Prepositions and other expressions of place (3)	62
Unità	27	Time prepositions (1)	63
Unità	28	Time prepositions (2)	65
Unità	29	Prepositions (1)	67
Unità	30	Prepositions (2)	69
Unità	31	Passato prossimo (1)	71
Unità	32	Passato prossimo (2)	73
Unità	33	Imperfect - form	76
Unità	34	Imperfect - use	78
Unità	35	Passato remoto	79

Contents

Unità 36	Imperfect	81
Unità 37	Future simple	83
Unità 38	Subject pronouns	85
Unità 39	Stressed object pronouns	87
Unità 40	Unstressed object pronouns	89
Unità 41	Reflexive verbs	91
Unità 42	*Ci* and *Ne*	93
Unità 43	The partitive *Ne*	95
Unità 44	Combined pronouns	97
Unità 45	Relative pronouns (1)	99
Unità 46	Relative pronouns (2)	101
Unità 47	Future perfect	103
Unità 48	Past perfect	105
Unità 49	Conditional - form	107
Unità 50	Conditional - use	109
Unità 51	Perfect conditional	110
Unità 52	*Stare* + gerund	112
Unità 53	*Stare per* + infinitive	113
Unità 54	Indefinite adjectives (1)	114
Unità 55	Indefinite adjectives (1) and pronouns	115
Unità 56	Indefinite pronouns	117
Unità 57	Quantifiers (1)	119
Unità 58	Quantifiers (2)	123
Unità 59	Comparative adjectives	125
Unità 60	Superlative adjectives (relativo and assoluto)	127
Unità 61	Irregular comparatives and superlatives - other forms	129
Unità 62	Comparative and superlative adverbs	131
Unità 63	Imperative - forms	133
Unità 64	Imperative with pronouns	135
Unità 65	Imperative - use	136
Unità 66	Present subjunctive - form	137
Unità 67	Imperfect subjunctive - form	140
Unità 68	Past and past perfect subjunctive - form	142
Unità 69	Subjunctive - use (1)	143
Unità 70	Subjunctive - use (2)	145

Contents

Unità 71	Sequence of tenses - with the indicative	147
Unità 72	Sequence of tenses - with the subjunctive (1)	149
Unità 73	Sequence of tenses - with the subjunctive (2)	151
Unità 74	Hypothetical clauses	153
Unità 75	The passive (1)	155
Unità 76	The passive (2) - *venire/andare*	157
Unità 77	Passive structures with *si*	159
Unità 78	Impersonal *si*	161
Unità 79	Impersonal structures with *loro, tu* and *uno*	163
Unità 80	Trapassato remoto	164
Unità 81	Reported speech (1)	165
Unità 82	Reported speech (2)	167
Unità 83	Reported speech (3)	169
Unità 84	Indefinite forms - present infinitive	172
Unità 85	Verbs/adjectives + di + infinitive	175
Unità 86	Verbs/adjectives + a + infinitive	177
Unità 87	*Da* & *per* + infinitive	179
Unità 88	Perfect infinitive	181
Unità 89	Other expressions with the infinitive	183
Unità 90	Indefinite forms - the gerund	185
Unità 91	Indefinite forms - participles	187
Unità 92	Coordinate conjunctions (1)	189
Unità 93	Coordinate conjunctions (2)	192
Unità 94	Subordinate conjunctions (1)	194
Unità 95	Subordinate conjunctions (2)	197
Unità 96	Modifying nouns and adjectives	200
Appendix 1	Italian phonetic symbols	203
Appendix 2	Italian vowels and consonants	204
Appendix 3	Glossary	207
Index		217
Diagnostic test		225
Answer Key		242

■ **Essere** (to be) is the *infinitive form* of the verb.

■ **Present indicative**

Affirmative form	
io	**sono**
tu	**sei**
(lui, lei)	**è**
(noi)	**siamo**
(voi)	**siete**
(loro)	**sono**

(Lui) **è** giapponese.
(He's Japanese.)

(Loro) **sono** a scuola.
(They're at school.)

For more information about the *present indicative*, see vedi Unità 3.

▶ Note: it is often unnecessary to use the subject pronoun (*io, tu, ecc.*) (*I, you, etc.*) See Unità 38 - *subject pronouns*. Do you know what is meant by *affirmative, negative, interrogative* and *interrogative-negative form*? See Appendix 3.

■ Study the pictures below.

(Lui) **non è** francese.
(He isn't French.)

(Loro) **non sono** in Germania.
(They aren't in Germany.)

The *negative* in Italian is formed by putting the word **non** before the verb.

■ Study the pictures below.

"Sei stanco?"
(Are you tired?)

"È una sedia?"
(Is it a chair?)

The *interrogative form* in Italian is expressed by the **intonation** of the sentence.
What does *intonation* mean? See Appendix 3.

■ The *interrogative-negative form* in Italian is expressed by the **intonation** of the sentence and the word **non** before the verb.

"Non è un fiore?"
(Isn't it a flower?)

"Non è un cane?"
(Isn't it a dog?)

the verb *avere* (infinitive - present indicative) 2

(io ho, tu hai, ecc.) (I have, you have, etc.)

■ **Avere** *(to have)* is the *infinitive form* of the verb.

■ **Present indicative**

Affirmative form	
io	**ho**
tu	**hai**
(lui, lei)	**ha**
(noi)	**abbiamo**
(voi)	**avete**
(loro)	**hanno**

*Carlo **ha** un gatto.*
(Carlo has (got) a cat.)

*Lucia e Antonio **hanno** un figlio.*
(Lucia e Antonio have (got) a son.)

For more information about *presente indicative*, see Unità 3.

▶ Note: it is often unnecessary to use the subject pronoun
(*io, tu,* etc.). See Unità 38 - subject pronouns.

Do you know what is meant by *affirmative, negative, interro-gative,* and *interrogative-negative*? See Appendix 3.

■ Study the sentences.

- (Io) **non ho** la macchina.
  (I haven't got a car.)
- (Noi) **non abbiamo** amici in Germania.
  (We haven't got any friends in Germany.)

The *negative form* in Italian is made by putting the word **non** before the verb.

■ Study the following sentences.

"Hai una sigaretta?"   *(Have you got a cigarette?)*

2

The *interrogative form* in Italian is expressed by the **intonation** of the sentence.

What does *intonation* mean? See Appendix 3.

■ The *interrogative-negative form* in Italian is expressed by the **intonation** of the sentence and the word **non** before the veb.

"Non avete il giornale di oggi?"
(Haven't you got today's newspaper?)

■ Look at the pictures.

Some common Italian expressions using the verb **avere**. Here are some examples.

avere fame	(to be hungry)
avere sete	(to be thirsty)
avere freddo	(to be cold)
avere paura	(to be afraid)
avere sonno	(to be sleepy)
avere caldo	(to be hot)
avere 20/30/40 anni	(to be 20/30/40 years old)

► The letter **h** in the words *ho, hai, ha, hanno* is silent. This is because in Italian the letter **h** is not an autonomous sound and is only used to write some words or sounds.

present indicative (1) (regular verbs)

(io amo, tu vedi, ecc.) (I love, you see, etc.)

3

■ Italian verbs can be divided into three groups:

I -are;	**II -ere;**	**III-ire.**
(cantare)	**(vedere)**	**(sentire - finire)**

■ Verbs belonging to group III-ire are divided into two further groups **III a (sentire)** e **III b (finire)**, due to some variations in endings; for example: tu sent**i**, tu fin**isci**.

I - ARE: cantare *(sing)*		**II - ERE: vedere** *(see)*	
io	cant - **o**	io	ved - **o**
tu	cant - **i**	tu	ved - **i**
(lui, lei)	cant - **a**	(lui, lei)	ved - **e**
(noi)	cant - **iamo**	(noi)	ved - **iamo**
(voi)	cant - **ate**	(voi)	ved - **ete**
(loro)	cant - **ano**	(loro)	ved - **ono**

III a - IRE: sentire *(hear)*		**III b - IRE: finire** *(finish)*	
io	sent - **o**	io	fin - **isc -o**
tu	sent - **i**	tu	fin - **isc -i**
(lui, lei)	sent - **e**	(lui, lei)	fin - **isc -e**
(noi)	sent - **iamo**	(noi)	fin - **iamo**
(voi)	sent - **ite**	(voi)	fin - **ite**
(loro)	sent - **ono**	(loro)	fin - **isc -ono**

▶ Note: It is often unnecessary to use the subject pronoun (*io, tu, ecc.*). See Unità 38 - *subject pronouns.*

What is meant by regular or irregular verbs? See Appendix 3.

■ Here is a list of the most common verbs belonging to group III:
III a aprire, coprire, divertirsi, dormire, offrire, partire, seguire, servire, soffrire, vestire.
(open, cover, enjoy oneself, sleep, offer, leave, follow, serve/ need, suffer, dress.)

III b capire, colpire, costruire, fornire, guarire, preferire, pulire, sostituire, spedire, unire.
(understand, hit, build, supply, get better, prefer, clean, substitute, send, join.)

■ For the *negative form* (- Io non ascolto musica classica.) (*I don't listen to classical music.*), *question form* (- Giochiamo a carte?) (*Shall we play cards?*) and *negative-question form* (- Non parli inglese?) (*Don't you speak English?*), see Unità 1 and 2.

■ Study the following examples:
  A) - La segretaria **comincia** a lavorare alle 9.
      (The secretary starts work at 9 o'clock)
  B) - Sandro **ascolta** la musica. *(Sandro is listening to music)*
  C) - Domani il Sig. Di Stefano **parte** per le vacanze.
      (Mr Di Stefano is going on holiday tomorrow)

The **present indicative** is used to describe an action
        A) that takes place habitually;
        B) that takes place at the moment of speaking;
        C) with future meaning.

■ Look at the position of the **word stress** in the present indicative:

	verbs with 1st person singular with two sillables	verbs with 1st person singular with more than two sillables
singular	parlo parli parla	rispondo rispondi risponde
plural	parliamo parlate parlano	rispondiamo rispondete rispondono

▶ For the third person plural (*loro*) the word stress goes as far back as possible, towards the beginning of the word, sometimes even on the fourth syllable from the end, for example: anticipano, or on the third from the end: parlano.

What is meant by the words *syllable* and *word stress*?
See Appendix 3.

present indicative (2) (irregular verbs)
(io vado, tu vai, ecc.) (I go, you go, etc.)

■ The most common irregular verbs in the present indicative:

potere (can)	volere (want)	dovere (must)	sapere (know)
posso	voglio	devo	so
puoi	vuoi	devi	sai
può	vuole	deve	sa
possiamo	vogliamo	dobbiamo	sappiamo
potete	volete	dovete	sapete
possono	vogliono	devono	sanno
piacere (like)	**bere** (drink)	**andare** (go)	**stare** (be, stay)
piaccio	bevo	vado	sto
piaci	bevi	vai	stai
piace	beve	va	sta
piacciamo	beviamo	andiamo	stiamo
piacete	bevete	andate	state
piacciono	bevono	vanno	stanno
fare (do, make)	**dare** (give)	**dire** (say)	**uscire** (go out)
faccio	do	dico	esco
fai	dai	dici	esci
fa	dà	dice	esce
facciamo	diamo	diciamo	usciamo
fate	date	dite	uscite
fanno	danno	dicono	escono

■ Numerous verbs such as *contenere* (*contain*), *comporre* (*make up*), *ritrarre* (*withdraw*) and *intervenire* (*intervene*) originate from the following verbs:

tenere *(keep)*	**porre** *(put, set)*	**trarre** *(draw)*	**venire** *(come)*
tengo*	pongo*	traggo	vengo*
tieni	poni	trai	vieni
tiene	pone	trae	viene
teniamo	poniamo	traiamo	veniamo
tenete	ponete	traete	venite
tengono	pongono*	traggono	vengono*

▶ * Some common verbs add a **g** to the stem only with *io* and *loro*. See **tenere**, **porre** and **venire**.
The most common of such verbs are: *rimanere* (*stay*), *salire* (*go up*) and *valere* (*be worth*).

■ Verbs that end in **-cere** and **-gere**.
Before **-o** and **-ono** they change from [tʃ] to [k] and from [dʒ] to [g].

vincere *(win)*		**leggere** *(read)*	
vinco	[vinko]	leggo	[ˈlɛggo]
vinci	[vintʃi]	leggi	[ˈlɛddʒi]
vince		legge	
vinciamo		leggiamo	
vincete		leggete	
vincono		leggono	

Do you know the phonetic symbols?
See Appendix 1.

■ Do you know what is meant by *vowels* and *consonants*?
See Appendix 3

	singular		plural	
masculine				
before a consonant	**il**	il cane	**i**	i cani
before S + consonant Z, PS, GN, X	**lo**	lo studente lo zio lo psicologo lo gnomo lo xenofobo	**gli**	gli studenti gli zii gli psicologi gli gnomi gli xenofobi
before a vowel	**l'**	l'albero l'indiano	**gli**	gli alberi gli indiani
feminine				
before a consonant	**la**	la casa	**le**	le case
before a vowel	**l'**	l'acqua	**le**	le acque

■ The definite article changes according to whether the noun
is feminine, masculine, singular or plural.

■ The definite article always comes before the noun.

■ The definite article is used

● when a noun is defined, in other words described or already referred to and known about:

● with abstract nouns:

*Ecco **la** ragazza che mi piace.*
(There's the girl I like.)

L'amore è un sentimento bellissimo.
(Love is beautiful feeling.)

● with nouns that indicate a category or species:
  – **Il** vino si fa con l'uva. *(Wine is made from grapes.)*

● with continents, countries (almost all), regions, seas, rivers and lakes, but rarely with the names of towns or cities:
  – **L'**Europa è un continente. *(Europe is a continent.)*
  – Bologna è vicino a Ferrara. *(Bologna is near Ferrara.)*

● with names and titles: Signore, Signora, Professore, Dottore, etc., but never when you speak directly to a person:

*Guarda **la** Signora Giovanna!*

Buongiorno, Signora Giovanna!

■ See Unità 11 for the use of the definite article with possessive adjectives and pronouns. See Unità 23 for the use of combined prepositions with the definite article.

▶ The definite article is not used in common expressions with the verb **avere**:
avere caldo/freddo, avere fame/sete, avere sonno, avere paura, etc.

	singular		plural	
masculine				
before a consonant	**un**	un cane	**dei**	dei cani
before S + consonant Z, PS, GN, X	**uno**	uno studente uno zio uno psicologo uno gnomo uno xenofobo	**degli**	degli studenti degli zii degli psicologi degli gnomi gli xenofobi
before a vowel	**un**	un albero un indiano	**degli**	degli alberi degli indiani
feminine				
before a consonant	**una**	una casa	**delle**	delle case
before a vowel	**un'**	un'italiana	**delle**	delle italiane

Study the picture.

*Vorrei **un** libro di poesie in inglese, per favore!*
(I'd like a poetry book in English, please!)

■ The indefinite article is used when the noun has not been defined or specified.

Compare with the use of the definite article: Unità 5.

■ The indefinite article always comes *before* the noun.

■ The indefinite article changes according to whether the noun is feminine or masculine.

■ **Un, uno, una, un'** are only used before singular nouns.

■ The forms **dei/degli/delle** are often used with the plural forms of nouns:

– Ho **degli** amici francesi che non vedo da anni.
(I've got some French friends that I haven't seen for years)

See Unità 23 for the use of combined prepositions with the definite article.

nouns and gender

(maschile, femminile) (masculine, feminine)

■ Nouns ending in **-O** are usually *masculine*:   **il** bambin**o**.

■ Nouns ending in **-A** are usually *feminine*:   **la** bambin**a**.

■ Nouns ending in **-E** can be either *masculine* or *feminine*:

masculine	*feminine*
il professore, **il** padre, **il** cane,	**la** chiave, **la** madre,
il pane, **il** dottore	**la** pace, **la** classe.

■ Some nouns ending in **-A** are *masculine*:

● some of these end in **-MA**:   **il** proble**ma**, **il** te**ma**, **il** cine**ma**, **il** siste**ma**, **il** program**ma**, **il** cli**ma**,

● a few end in **-ista**:   **l'**arti**sta**, **il** denti**sta**, **il** giornali**sta**,

● others indicate a male figure: **il** poeta, **il** pilota.

■ Nouns with the following endings are usually *masculine*:
- **-ORE**   **il** fi**ore**
- **-ONE**   **il** sap**one**
- **-ALE**   **il** giorn**ale**
- **-ILE**   **il** fuc**ile**

■ Nouns that end with a consonant are usually *masculine*. These mostly derive from foreign words: **il** bar, **lo** sport.

■ Some nouns ending in **-O** are *feminine*. These are often words that have been shortened:
la radio, **la** foto, **la** moto, **l'**auto, **la** mano
i.e. **la** foto = **la** fotografia.

■ Nouns ending in **-TÀ** and in **-TÙ** are *feminine*:

> **la** libertà, **la** gioventù.

■ Nouns ending in **-I** are usually *feminine*:

> **la** crisi, **l'**analisi, **la** sintesi.

■ Nouns with the following endings are usually *feminine*:

-IONE	**la** lezione
-IE	**la** serie
-ICE	**la** lavatrice

■ Names of **continents, countries, regions, islands, towns and cities** are usually *feminine*.

■ Names of **mountains, lakes, rivers,** and **seas** are usually *masculine*.

■ **The months of the year** and **days of the week** are always *masculine*.

▶ Exception to the rule: **la** domenica.

	singular		plural	
masculine	-O	il telefono	-I	i telefoni
	-E	il cane	-I	i cani
	-A	il sistema	-I	i sistemi
feminine	-A	la scuola	-E	le scuole
	-E	la chiave	-I	le chiavi
	-TÀ	la libertà	-TÀ	le libertà
	-TÙ	la virtù	-TÙ	le virtù
	-I	la crisi	-I	le crisi
	-O	la mano	-I	le mani

Nouns that do not change:

	singular	plural
nouns ending with a consonant, and foreign words in general	**il** film	**i** film
monosyllable nouns	**il** re	**i** re
shortened nouns	**la** foto	**le** foto

	singular		**plural**	
masculine	-IO	il figlio	-I	i figli
	-IO	lo zio	-II	gli zii
	-CO -GO *(accent on the second syllable from the end)*	il cuoco /ˈkwɔko/ l'albergo /alˈbɛrgo/	-CHI -GHI *(accent on the second syllable from the end)*	i cuochi /ˈkwɔki/ gli alberghi /alˈbɛrgi/
	-CO -GO *(accent on the third syllable from the end)*	il medico /ˈmɛdiko/ lo psicologo /psiˈkɔlogo/	-CI -GI *(accent on the third syllable from the end)*	i medici /ˈmɛditʃi/ gli psicologi /psiˈkɔlodʒi/
feminine	-CA -GA	la banca la droga	-CHE -GHE	le banche le droghe
	-CIA	la farmacia	-CIE	le farmacie
	-CIA -GIA *(after a vowel)*	la camicia la valigia	-CIE -GIE *(after a vowel)*	le camicie le valigie
	-CIA -GIA *(after a consonant)*	l'arancia la pioggia	-CE -GE *(after a consonant)*	le arance le piogge

▶ Many nouns ending in **-co** and **-go** do not follow the given plural rule, e.g.: l'ami**co**, gli ami**ci**.

Can you remember the phonetic symbols? See Appendix 1.
Can you remember how to write the sounds /tʃo/, /ki/, etc. in Italian? See Appendix 2.

the plural forms of nouns (2)
irregular plurals
(l'uomo, gli uomini) (the man, the men)

9

The following nouns have irregular plural forms:

singular		plural
l'uomo	*man*	gli uomini
il dio	*god*	gli dei
l'uovo	*egg*	le uova
il paio	*pair*	le paia

Some parts of the body are masculine in the singular form, but feminine in the plural form:

singular		plural
il ginocchio	*knee*	le ginocchia
il braccio	*arm*	le braccia
il dito	*finger*	le dita
il sopracciglio	*eyebrow*	le sopracciglia
l'osso	*bone*	le ossa
il labbro	*lip*	le labbra

Some very common nouns are only used in the plural form:

i pantaloni	*trousers*
le mutande	*briefs*
gli occhiali	*glasses*

Some very common nouns are only used in the singular form:

la gente	*people*
la frutta	*fruit*
la fame	*hunger*
la sete	*thirst*

■

		singular		plural
masculine	-O	il bambino bravo	-I	i bambini bravi
	-E	l'esercizio facile	-I	gli esercizi facili
feminine	-A	la bambina brava	-E	le bambine brave
	-E	la lezione facile	-I	le lezioni facili

■ Adjectives ending in **-A**:

masculine plural changes to **-I**:   **Il** simbol**o** socialist**a**
                                                  I simbol**i** socialist**i**
                                                  (The socialist symbols)

feminine plural changes to **-E**:   **La** politic**a** liberist**a**
                                                  Le politic**he** liberist**e**
                                                  (Liberalist politics)

■ Adjectives ending in **-co** and **-go** follow the same rules as nouns that end in **-co** and **-go**. See Unità 8.

■ Adjectives can be placed **before** or **after** a noun.
If the adjective is longer than the noun it is usually positioned *after* the noun.

■ The adjectives **bello**, **quello** and **buono**
If the adjectives **bello** or **quello** are placed *before* the noun, they follow the rules of the *definite article*.

	singular		
masculine	**il** bambino	**il bel** bambino	**quel** bambino
	lo stadio	**il bello** stadio	**quello** stadio
	l'albero	**il bell'**albero	**quell'**albero
feminine	**la** ragazza	**la bella** ragazza	**quella** ragazza
	l'idea	**la bell'**idea	**quell'**idea

	plural		
masculine	**i** bambini	**i bei** bambini	**quei** bambini
	gli stadii	**i begli** stadi	**quegli** stadii
	gli alberi	**i begli** alberi	**quegli** alberi
feminine	**le** ragazze	**le belle** ragazze	**quelle** ragazze
	le idee	**le belle** idee	**quelle** idee

■ The adjective **buono** follows the rules of the *indefinite article*.

	singular	
masculine	**un** bambino	**un buon** bambino
	uno studente	**un buono** studente
feminine	**un** artista	**un buon** artista
	una ragazza	**una buona** ragazza
	un'amica	**una buon'**amica

▶ If **bello** or **buono** are placed *after* the noun they act like normal **-A** or **-O** ending adjectives:
  – Mio figlio è un bimb**o** buon**o**, non piange quasi mai.
    (My son is a really good baby, he hardly ever cries.)
  – In questo bosco ci sono tanti alber**i** bell**i**.
    (There are lots of lovely trees in this forest.)

Quello as a demonstrative adjective, see Unità 12.
Quello as a demonstrative pronoun, see Unità 13.

■ Study the following sentence.

– Parma è una città **molto tranquilla**.
(Parma is a very quiet town).

The adjective (3) is always placed after the noun (1) when it is modified by an adverb (2):

(1)   (2)   (3)

– Ecco un monumento **estremamente interessante**.
(Now there's an extremely interesting monument)

■ Possessive adjectives and possessive pronouns have the same form.

	masculine		feminine	
	singular	**plural**	**singular**	**plural**
I pers. sing.	**mio**	**miei**	**mia**	**mie**
II pers. sing.	**tuo**	**tuoi**	**tua**	**tue**
III pers. sing.	**suo**	**suoi**	**sua**	**sue**
I pers. plur.	**nostro**	**nostri**	**nostra**	**nostre**
II pers. plur.	**vostro**	**vostri**	**vostra**	**vostre**
III pers. plur.	**loro**	**loro**	**loro**	**loro**

■ Study the following sentences.
– **Il** mio amico Fulvio è medico.*(My friend Fulvio is a doctor.)*
– **La** mia amica Anne è francese.*(My friend Anne is French.)*

The possessives change according to gender and number of the possessed noun.
E.g.: if the noun is masculine and singular (ami**co**), the possessive form is **il** mi**o**.

▶ **Loro** does not change form. – Ecco là **le loro** ragazze.
(Their girlfriends are over there)

■ How do you distinguish between a **possessive adjective** and a **possessive pronoun**?

The possessive adjective is followed by the noun that is being referred to.
The possessive pronoun replaces the noun.

Possessive adjectives (before a noun).
– **La mia casa** ha tre piani. *(My house is on three floors.)*
– **Il loro cane** è molto pericoloso con gli estranei.
(Their dog is very aggressive towards strangers.)

Possessive pronouns (substitute a noun):
- **La casa** di Mario ha sette piani, **la mia** tre.
  (Mario's house is on seven floors, mine is on three.)
- **Il cane** del Signor Bianchi non fa male mai a nessuno, invece **il loro** è molto pericoloso.
  (Mr Bianchi's dog never hurts anyone, but theirs is very dangerous.)

▶ In some cases the possessive adjective is placed **after** the noun. For example:
- Vieni a casa mia stasera?
  (Are you coming to my house this evening?)
- Mamma mia! *(My goodness!)*

▪ The *definite article* is usually required before possessive adjectives and pronouns.

● The definite article is generally *omitted* with *singular* nouns referring to members of the family (*padre, madre, sorella,* etc.) but required when used in the *plural* form.
- **Mia** madre si chiama Paola. *(My mother's name is Paola.)*
- **I miei** nonni sono molto vecchi. *(My grandparents are very old.)*

▶ With **loro** the article is required even when nouns refer to the family:
- **La loro** madre è molto giovane. *(Their mother is very young)*

▪ **Proprio** is used instead of **suo** and **loro** when

● the subject is *nessuno, tutti* (*no one, everyone*) or other *indefinite pronouns.* (See Appendix 3):
- **Nessuno** deve pensare solo ai **propri** affari.
  (No one should think only about their own interests.)

● when the subject is not mentioned, in other words the sentence construction is impersonal (See Appendix 3):
- **È** importante ripensare ai **propri** errori.
  (It is important to reconsider your own mistakes.)

demonstrative adjectives

(questo libro, quella casa) (this book, that house)

■ Demonstrative adjectives: **questo**

	singular *this*		**plural** *these*
masculine	*before a consonant* **questo**	*before a vowel* **quest'**	**questi**
feminine	*before a consonant* **questa**	*before a vowel* **quest'**	**queste**

■ **Quello**

	singular *that*		**plural** *those*	
masculine				
before a consonant	**quel**	quel bambino	**quei**	quei bambini
before S + consonant Z, PS, GN, X	**quello**	quello studente	**quegli**	quegli studenti
before a vowel	**quell'**	quell'albero	**quegli**	quegli alberi
feminine				
before a consonant	**quella**	quella casa	**quelle**	quelle case
before a vowel	**quell'**	quell'ape	**quelle**	quelle api

▶ **Quello** used as an *adjective* behaves like the definite article (See Unità 5) and the adjective **bello** (See Unità 10).

■ Study the picture.

Questo bambino è mio figlio Claudio.

Questo is used for people and things which are *close* to the speaker.

■ Study the picture.

Quel bambino è mio figlio Claudio.

Quello is used for people and things which are at a *distance* from the speaker.

▶ *The article is not* used with the demonstrative adjectives.

■ Apart from **questo** and **quello** there are other less common demonstrative adjectives such as:
codesto used in some regions of Italy or in bureaucratic language to talk about an object at a *distance* from the speaker but *close* to the listener.
– Egregio Direttore, mi rivolgo a **codesto** Istituto per...
(Dear Sir, I am writing to this Institute in order to...)

■ **Demonstrative pronouns: questo e quello** (*this, that*)

	singular *this/that*	**plural** *these/those*
masculine	questo	questi
	quello	quelli
feminine	questa	queste
	quella	quelle

■ The *demonstrative pronouns* take the place of a noun:

Questo bambino è mio figlio Claudio e questo è mio nipote Antonio.

Quel bambino è mio figlio Claudio e quello che gioca con lui è un suo amico.

▶ The *article* is *not* used with the demonstrative pronouns.

■ Study the picture.

Preferisci i film d'avventura o i film comici?

Quelli d'avventura.

The pronoun **quello** - but not *questo* - is used to avoid the repetition of a noun.

■ Study the picture.

Cosa ti piace fare nel tempo libero?

Leggere libri, soprattutto **quelli che** mi consigliano gli amici.

Quello - but not *questo* - is used before relative pronouns.

■ Apart from *questo* and *quello* there are other less common demonstrative pronouns:

● **codesto**: used in some regions of Italy or in bureaucratic language to talk about an object at a distance from the speaker but *close* to the listener.

● **ciò**: used instead of *quello* or *questo* when the meaning is *questa* or *quella* cosa. *(This or that thing/what)*.

– **Ciò** (quello) **che** mi dici mi rende felice!
(What you're telling me makes me very happy!)

vorrei e *potrei* (*would like* and *could*) **14**

(vorrei una birra, per favore, ecc.) (I'd like a beer, please, etc.)

■ **Vorrei** (*would like*) is used to express a wish or offer something, while **potrei** (*could*) is used to ask for permission or to make a request.

vorr**ei**	potr**ei**
vorr**esti**	potr**esti**
vorr**ebbe**	potr**ebbe**
vorr**emmo**	potr**emmo**
vorr**este**	potr**este**
vorr**ebbero**	potr**ebbero**

▶ These verb endings belong to the *conditional*.
See Unità 49 and 50.

■ Study the picture.

1) What would like to eat? I'd like a plate of spaghetti with a tuna sauce, please.

2) Giovanni and Sandra would like to go to the seaside on Sunday. What would you like to do? I'm not sure yet.

3) This seat is free, isn't it? Could I sit here, please? Of course!

4) Could you tell me where the station is, please?

cardinal numbers
(uno, due, tre, ecc.) (one, two, three, etc.)

■ The cardinal numbers:

0 zero	**17** diciassette	**70** settanta
1 uno	**18** diciotto	**80** ottanta
2 due	**19** diciannove	**90** novanta
3 tre	**20** venti	**100** cento
4 quattro	**21** ventuno	**102** centodue
5 cinque	**22** ventidue	**200** duecento
6 sei	**23** ventitré	**1.000** mille
7 sette	**24** ventiquattro	**2.000** duemila
8 otto	**25** venticinque	**10.000** diecimila
9 nove	**26** ventisei	**100.000** centomila
10 dieci	**27** ventisette	**1.000.000** un milione
11 undici	**28** ventotto	**1.000.000.000** un miliardo
12 dodici	**29** ventinove	
13 tredici	**30** trenta	
14 quattordici	**40** quaranta	
15 quindici	**50** cinquanta	
16 sedici	**60** sessanta	

■ When a cardinal number is used as an adjective it is usually placed before the noun it is referring to.
  – Questo libro ha **trecentoventidue** pagine.
  (This book has three hundred and twenty-two pages.)

■ The cardinal numbers are invariable except in the following cases:

● **uno** has a feminine form: **una;**
  – Guarda, **una** stella cadente! *(Look! A shooting star!)*

● **mille** has an irregular plural form: **mila;**
  – Questa casa costa circa **quattrocentomila** euro.
  (This house costs about four hundred thousand euro.)

- **zero**, **milione** and **miliardo** all have regular plural forms:
  cinque zeri (*five noughts*), **due milioni** (*two million*),
  tre miliardi (*three billion*).

X	= per
:	= diviso
-	= meno
+	= più
=	= uguale

  – Secondo un rapporto dell'Organizzazione
    Mondiale della Sanità nel 2020 saranno sette miliardi
    gli esseri umani con problemi derivanti dalla malnutrizione.
  – *According to a report by the World Health Organization,
    in the year 2020 seven billion people will be suffering from
    problems caused by malnutrition.)*

■ The cardinal numbers are written as one word, except for
  the figures with **milione** and **miliardo**; in these cases the
  words are written separately with an **e** (*and*) between the
  two numbers.

  – Quella villa è molto cara, costa un **milione** e **duecentomila** euro.
    *(That villa is very expensive, it costs one million two
    hundred thousand euro.)*

► When writing a cheque the numbers are written together as
  one word without using an **e** (*and*). This includes amounts
  with the words **milioni** and **miliardi**.

■ When the words **milione** and **miliardo** are followed by a
  noun, the preposition **di** is used.
  – Milano ha circa due milioni **di** abitanti.
    (Milan has about two million inhabitants.)

■ Numbers in Italian are masculine.
  – **Il cinque** è il mio numero fortunato.
    (Five is my lucky number.)

16 ordinal numbers

(primo, secondo, ecc.) (first, second, etc.)

■ The ordinal numbers:

1°	primo	*(first)*	11°	undicesimo
2°	secondo	*(second)*	12°	dodicesimo
3°	terzo	*(third)*	13°	tredicesimo
4°	quarto	*(fourth)*	20°	ventesimo
5°	quinto	*(fifth)*	21°	ventunesimo
6°	sesto	*(sixth etc.)*	22°	ventiduesimo
7°	settimo		23°	ventitreesimo
8°	ottavo		100°	centesimo
9°	nono		1.000°	millesimo
10°	decimo		1.000.000°	milionesimo

■ When an ordinal number is used as an adjective it is usually placed *before* the noun it is referring to:
– Abito al **terzo** piano. *(I live on the third floor.)*

▶ The ordinal numbers are placed *after* the names of kings, popes, etc.:
– Ecco il ritratto dell'imperatore Carlo **V**.
(There's the portrait of the Emperor Charles V.)

■ The ordinal numbers are formed by adding the ending **-esimo** to the cardinal number, remembering to remove the final vowel of the number: ventiquattr**e**simo.

▶ With the number **-tre** the final vowel is kept: ventitr**ee**simo.

■ Ordinal numbers have *masculine*, *feminine*, *singular* and *plural* forms, like normal adjectives ending in **-o** and **-a**:

– Prenda **la** secon**da** strad**a** a destra!
  (Take the second street on your right!)

▢ Fractions are formed by using a *cardinal* number followed by an *ordinal* number:

2/3 = due terzi *(two thirds)*
5/11 = cinque undicesimi *(five elevenths)*

► Exception: 1/2 = un mezzo *(a half)*

▢ When you want to talk about an approximate quantity, without stating a precise number, the following words are used:

una decina = circa dieci *(about ten)*
una ventina, trentina, ecc. = circa venti, trenta, ecc. *(about twenty, thirty, etc.)*
un centinaio, un migliaio = circa cento, mille *(about a hundred, a thousand)*

Plural: alcune decine, centinaia, migliaia *(tens, hundreds, thousands)*

■ There are two ways of telling the time: one is used in everyday Italian and the other for more official situations (times of trains, planes, cinema, theatre, radio and TV programmes, etc.).

■ Look at the example below. Can you work out the rule?

le due e dieci

le dieci e cinque

l'una e venti

le sette meno cinque

le otto meno venti

le due e dieci
le dieci e cinque
le tredici e venti
le diciotto e cinquantacinque
le diciannove e quaranta

● For official times the twenty-four hour clock is used, i.e. 19.00 "*le diciannove*". 20.50 "*le venti e cinquanta*"; while in more colloquial situations it is more common to say *le sette*, *le nove meno dieci*.

● When telling the time cardinal numbers are used (uno, due, tre, ecc.).

● When telling the time the plural form of the verb is used:
- **Sono le** due e dieci, le undici e cinque, le otto meno venti, etc. *(It's ten past two, five past eleven, twenty to eight, etc.).*

▶ The single form of the verb is required only in one case:
- **È l'**una, l'una e cinque, l'una meno venti, etc.
(It's one o'clock, five past one, twenty to one, etc.).

● When telling the time the *definite article* (il, lo, la, etc.) is always needed before the number on the hour.

- Sono **le** tre.   (It's three o'clock.)
- È l'una e dieci.   (It's ten past one.)

■ You can ask the time in various ways. Two very common forms are:
Che ore è?   Che ore sono?   *(What's the time?)*

■ **Mezzogiorno** and **mezzanotte** (midday and midnight):

1 - È mezzogiorno = ore 12.00 *(It's midday.)*
2 - È mezzanotte = ore 24.00 *(It's midnight.)*

With **mezzogiorno** and **mezzanotte** the singular form of the verb is used and the article is omitted.

▶ In official situations the following forms are used:
1 - Sono le dodici.   2 - Sono le ventiquattro.
  (It's twelve o'clock.)   (It's twenty-four hundred hours.)

■ Tra le ore e i minuti occorre normalmente mettere
e before the half hour: 6.25 sei **e** venticinque
                (twenty-five past six)

meno dopo la mezz'ora: 11.40 dodici **meno** venti
                (twenty to twelve)

■ For the following times you say:

2.15	**due e un quarto**	*(a quarter past two)*
2.30	**due e mezza**	*(half past two)*
2.45	**tre meno un quarto** *	*(a quarter to three)*

▶ * Sometimes *due **e tre** quarti* or *un quarto **alle** tre* are used. The form with **meno** is frequently substituted by **alle**:

5.50	dieci **alle** sei	*(ten to six)*
9.40	venti **alle** dieci	*(twenty to ten)*

■ The preposition used with time expressions is **a/alle/all'**; see Unità 23.

– **A** mezzogiorno in estate fa molto caldo.
  (It is very hot in summer at midday.)
– Vado sempre a letto **alle** undici e mezza.
  (I always go to bed at half past eleven.)
– Pranzo solitamente **all'**una e un quarto.
  (I usually have lunch at a quarter past one.)

dates, years and centuries
(30 dicembre 1995 - XX secolo)
(30th December 1995 - 20th century)

18

■ Study the pictures.

Buongiorno a tutti, sono le otto e venti del 10 febbraio 2003...

To talk about the **date** cardinal numbers are used:

Oggi è il **nove** ottobre 2003.
(Today it 9th of October 2003.)

▶ Except for when it is the first day of the month:

Il **primo** maggio è la Festa del Lavoro.
(The first of May is May Day.)

■ Look at the picture.

What preposition do you use with the date? **No preposition** is needed with the **date**. See Unità 27.

■ The **year** is usually written in numbers but said as *one word*.

1995 ⟶ **millenovecentonovantacinque**

or you can use an *abbreviated* form if it is clear which century is being referred to:

– L'89 (l'**ottantanove**) è stato l'anno della caduta del muro di Berlino. *('89 was the year the Berlin wall fell.)*

■ When referring to a decade, for example the years between 1980 and 1989, you can say:
Gli anni Ottanta *(The Eighties)*

■ You can talk about **centuries** in two ways, either using the **cardinal numbers** (for centuries after the year one thousand) usually written with a capital letter:

– Il **Quattrocento** è il secolo del Rinascimento in Italia.
    ↓   *(The fifteenth century is the period of*
   1400   *the Renaissance in Italy.)*

or with ordinal numbers:
– Il **quindicesimo** secolo è il secolo del Rinascimento in Italia.
    ↓   *(The fifteenth century is the period of*
   1400   *the Renaissance in Italy.)*

■ With **years** and **centuries** the preposition **in** is used in its combined form with the article **nel/nell'**. See Unità 23 and 27.

– Mi sono sposato **nel** 1992. *(I got married in 1992).*
– Colombo "scoprì" l'America **nel** quindicesimo secolo
(**nel** Quattrocento).
(Columbus "discovered" America in the fifteenth century)
(in the fourteen hundreds.)
– **Nell'**Ottocento l'Italia era un paese molto povero.
(In the eighteen hundreds Italy was a very poor country.)

question words (1)
(che?, che cosa?, ecc.) (who?, what?, etc.)

19

CHI? *(Who?)*

Study the pictures.

Chi is used to ask about a person's identity. It is invariable and only used for people.

■ Question words can follow prepositions, e.g.: **DI CHI?** *(Whose?)*

Chi è quella ragazza?

È la ragazza di Pietro

Di chi è questa penna?

È di Giorgio.

CHE COSA? *(What?)*

Che cosa is invariable and only used for things.

Che cosa mangiamo oggi?

Ti va una pizza?

▶ **Che** or **cosa** can be used instead of **Che cosa.**
  – **Che** mangiamo oggi? **Cosa** mangiamo oggi?
  (What are we going to eat today?).

QUALE? *(Which? What?)*

Quale becomes **quali** in plural form.

"Tre croci" di Tozzi, è molto carino!

Quale libro stai leggendo?

▶ **Che** can be used instead of **quale**.
  – **Che** libro stai leggendo?
  (What book are you reading?)

▶ before **è qual** is used.
  – **Qual** è l'indirizzo della tua scuola?
  (What's the address of your school?)

QUANTO?   *(How much? how many? etc.)*

Quanto changes with gender and number. It is used to ask about **quantity**. It acts as a pronoun and an adjective.

Do you remember the difference between an adjective and a pronoun? See Appendix 3.

adjective
Quanto tempo ci vuole da Roma a Napoli in treno? *(How long does is take from Rome to Naples by train?)*
Quanta carne mangi alla settimana? *(How much meat do you eat a week?)*
Quanti amici hai in Italia? *(How many friends have you got in Italy?)*
Quante sigarette fumi ogni giorno? *(How many cigarettes do you smoke a day?)*

pronoun
Quanto costa la tua nuova macchina? *(How much is your new car?)*
Per quanti hai preparato stasera? *(How many people have you cooked for tonight?)*

question words (2) and exclamation

20

(perché?, dove?, quanto!, ecc.) (why?, where?, what a...!, etc.)

COME?   *(How?)*

Come is used to ask about the **way** something is done or the **way** someone feels. Study the picture.

*Ciao Carla! **Come** va? **Come sei** arrivata a Torino?*

*In macchina con Cristina, e tu **come** stai?*

PERCHÉ?   *(Why?)*

Perché is used to ask for a **reason**:
"**Perché** non mi hai chiamato ieri sera?"
"**Perché** sono tornata a casa alle due questa notte".
*("Why didn't you call me yesterday evening?"
"Because I got home at two o'clock in the morning.")*

▶ **Perché** is used for both the question and the answer.

QUANDO?   *(When?)*

Quando is used to ask about **time**:
"**Quando** sei tornata? Alle due?" "Sì, ma perché ti arrabbi?"
("When did you get back? At two o'clock?" "Yes, but why are you angry?")

DOVE?   *(Where?)*

Dove is used to ask about **place**, whether involving movement or state.
See Appendix 3: expressions of place.

DA DOVE? *(Where from?)*

Da dove is used to ask about a person's place of origin:

■ Some question words can be used to make exclamations.

CHE	QUANTO		COME

adverbs (1)
(facilmente, bene, ecc.) (easily, well, etc.)

21

■ Various groups of adverbs exist, some express **manner**, **quantity**, or **doubt**, others are used to **deny** or **confirm** something, etc.

■ Adverbs of manner are usually formed from the adjective. Look at the following table.

adjective	adverb formation feminine adjective form	adverb
fredd**o** (cold)	fredd**a** + mente	fredd**amente** (coldly)
breve (brief)	breve + mente	brev**emente** (briefly)
facil**e** (easy)	facil + mente	facil**mente** (easily)
regolar**e** (regular)	regolar + mente	regol**armente** (regular)

– Ieri ho visto Giovanna. Mi ha salutato molto **freddamente**.
  (I saw Giovanna yesterday. She said hello to me very coldly.)

▶ Some adverbs are irregular:

aggettivo	avverbio
buono (good)	**bene** (well)
cattivo (bad)	**male** (badly)
leggero (light, slight)	legger**mente** (lightly, sligtly)
violento (violent)	violent**emente** (violently)

– Sergio dice che l'esame è andato **bene**.
  (Sergio says the exam went well.)

■ **Confirming** and **denying** adverbs.
Apart from *sì* (yes), there are many other words that can be used to confirm something, e.g.
certamente, certo, sicuramente, davvero, esattamente, ecc.
(certainly, of course, surely, really, exactly, etc.)

To deny something, *no* and *non* are used. *Non* is followed
by a verb and the rest of the sentence.

- Sai nuotare?   - **No, non mi** piace bagnarmi.
  (*Can you swim?*   *No, I don't like getting wet.*)

► In colloquial language *non* can be made stronger by adding
  the word *mica*.
  Sei stato tu a rompere il vetro della finestra!
  (*It was you who broke the window!*)
  No, **non** è **mica** colpa mia; mi hanno spinto!
  (*No, it really wasn't my fault, they pushed me!*)

■ Adverbs espressing **doubt**.
  Forse, magari, probabilmente, ecc.
  (*maybe, perhaps, probably, etc.*)
  – Che cosa fai questo fine settimana?
  – Non lo so ancora. **Forse** domani sera esco con Davide o
    magari domenica lo invito a cena a casa mia.
    (*What are you doing this weekend? I'm not sure yet.
    Maybe I'll go out with Davide tomorrow evening or
    perhaps I'll invite him to dinner at my place on Sunday.*)

■ Study the position of the adverbs in the following examples.
  – Ho lavorato **duramente** questa settimana.
    (*I've worked hard this week.*)
  – Mi sembra che il tuo vestito sia **leggermente** corto.
    (*I think your dress is just slightly on the short-side.*)

Adverbs are usually placed *after* the verb. See Unità 22 for the
adverbs of frequency.

adverbs (2)
(molto, sempre, ecc.) (much, always, etc.)

22

■ Adverbs of **quantity**

+++	**molto, tanto, parecchio**	*very much, a lot (of), a load (of)*
++	**abbastanza, piuttosto**	*enough, quite, rather*
+	**un po'**	*a little*
-	**poco**	*little*
--	**niente**	*not... at all*

– Ho studiato **molto**; mi fa male la testa.
  (I've studied a lot; I've got a headache.)
– Fa già **abbastanza** caldo, domani vado al mare.
  (It's already quite warm, tomorrow I'm going to the seaside.)

● Study the picture.

*Hai bevuto **troppo** è meglio che ti accompagni a casa!*

Troppo *(too/too much)* is used to indicate excessiveness.

■ **Frequency** adverbs

sempre	*(always)*
quasi sempre	*(almost always)*
solitamente, normalmente	*(usually, normally)*
spesso	*(often)*
talvolta, a volte	*(sometimes, occasionally)*
raramente	*(rarely)*
quasi mai	*(hardly ever)*
mai	*(never)*

*Io ho **sempre** fame; tu invece non mangi **mai**. Come fai?*

■ Adverbs are usually placed *after* the verb.

Some adverbs of frequency (*mai, sempre, spesso, quasi mai, quasi sempre*) can be placed between the auxiliary verb and the past participle in compound tense forms:

– Ho **sempre** pensato che l'Italia fosse un paese di gente bassa e con i capelli scuri.
  (I always thought that Italy was a nation of small people with dark hair.)

– Non sono **quasi mai** andato in montagna da piccolo, ma adesso mi piace molto.
  (When I was small I hardly ever went to the mountains, but now I like going there a lot.)

■ See Unità 62 for the comparative form of the adverb.

■ Prepositions in Italian:
di *(of)*, **a** *(to, at)*, **da** *(from)*, **in** *(in)*, **con** *(with, by)*, **su** *(on)*,
per *(for)*, **tra/fra** *(among, between)*.

■ When the prepositions **a**, **da**, **di**, **in**, **su** are used together
with the definite article, compound words are formed.

	il	lo	l'	la	i	gli	le
a	al	allo	all'	alla	ai	agli	alle
da	dal	dallo	dall'	dalla	dai	dagli	dalle
di	del	dello	dell'	della	dei	degli	delle
in	nel	nello	nell'	nella	nei	negli	nelle
su	sul	sullo	sull'	sulla	sui	sugli	sulle

– Vai spesso **al** cinema?
 (Do you often go to the cinema?)

– **Nella** mia strada vivono molti stranieri.
 (Lots of foreigners live in my street.)

■ The preposition **con** may also have a form:

> con + il = **col** but also **con il**
> con + i = **coi** but also **con i**

In modern Italian it is more common to use **con il**/etc. instead
of the combined form:
> – Fa molto freddo. Esci **con il** cappotto!
> *(It's really cold. Put your coat on to go out!)*

■ **Prepositions of place and movement**
Do you understand these two concepts? See Appendix 3:
expressions of place.
For the use of the definite article, see Unità 5. For prepositions
with the definite article, see Unità 23.

IN   (In, at, to)

● To indicate position:
  – **Nel** tuo zaino ci sono troppi libri.
    (There are too many books in your rucksack.)

● With shops, places of work and public offices, etc:

  – Claudio è **in** ufficio. *(Claudio is in the office.)*
  – **Nella** macelleria di Piazza Garibaldi si può comprare
    dell'ottima carne.
    *(You can buy excellent meat at the butcher's in Piazza
    Garibaldi.)*
  – Stasera Sandra e io andiamo **in** pizzeria.
    (Sandra and I are going to the pizzeria tonight.)
  – I francobolli si comprano **in** posta o **in** tabaccheria.
    (You can buy stamps at the post-office or at the tobacconist's.)
  – Ogni domenica alle ore 10 vado alla messa **nella** chiesa
    di Sant'Antonio.
    (I go to mass at Sant'Antonio's every Sunday at 10 o'clock.)

▶ See Unità 25 **da** for the use of: vado **dal** macellaio/vado **in**
  macelleria. *(I'm going to the butcher's.)*

● With the names of continents, countries, regions and large
  islands:

▶ without the definite article:

- Chi viene **in** Europa ha la possibilità di visitare molti paesi ricchi di storia.
  (Those coming to Europe can visit many countries full of history.)
- Mi piacerebbe vivere **in** Portogallo per un po' di tempo.
  (I'd like to live in Portugal for a while.)
- **In** Emilia Romagna il tasso di disoccupazione è molto basso.
  (The rate of unemployment in Emilia Romagna is very low.)
- L'anno scorso ho trascorso le vacanze **in** Madagascar.
  (Last year I spent my holidays in Madagascar.)

● With the names of squares, roads, etc.:

▶ without the definite article:

- Abito **in** Via dei Pini. *(I live in Via dei Pini.)*
- **In** Piazza del Duomo a Parma ci sono opere artistiche di grande valore.
  (There are great works of art in Parma's Piazza del Duomo.)

▶ with parts of the house:

- Gianni è sceso **in** garage a pulire la bicicletta.
  (Gianni has gone down to the garage to clean his bike.)
- Preferisco mangiare con gli amici **in** soggiorno, perché **in** cucina c'è poco spazio.
  (I prefer eating in the living-room with my friends, as there isn't much room in the kitchen.)
- **Nei** bagni inglesi normalmente non c'è il bidè.
  (English bathrooms don't usually have bidets.)

● With the following expressions:

- **in** centro; **in** periferia; **in** campagna; **in** montagna.
  (in the centre; in the suburbs; in the country; in the mountains.)

A *(At, in)*

● With the names of cities, towns, villages and small islands:

  – Abito **a** Padova. *(I live in Padova.)*
  – Quest'anno vado **a** Spoleto per il festival.
    (I'm going to Spoleto for the festival this year.)
  – Non so cosa darei per vivere **all'**Isola d'Elba.
    (I'd give anything to live on Elba.)

● with the word **casa**:

  – Questa sera resto **a** casa.
    (I'm staying at home this evening.)
  – Domani siamo invitati a cena **a** casa di Carlo.
    (We've been invited to dinner at Carlo's house tomorrow.)

● Con le seguenti espressioni:

a scuola; **all'**università; **al** cinema; **a** teatro; **al** mercato;
al ristorante; **allo** stadio; **al** mare;
(at school; at university; at the cinema; at the theatre; at the market; at the restaurant; at the stadium; at the seaside;)
a destra; **a** sinistra; *(on the left; on the right;)*
all'estero; *(abroad)* **al** telefono. *(on the telephone.)*

■ **Movement - place of origin**

DA   *(From)*

- Vengo **da** Londra, la più bella città d'Europa.
  (I come from London, the most beautiful city in Europe.)
- Karl è tedesco, viene **da** Norimberga.
  (Karl is German, he comes from Nurnberg.)

▶ **DA** used together with a person's name or a profession or personal object pronoun takes on the meaning of **a casa di, nel negozio/ufficio/ecc. di**. *(at someone's house, shop, office, etc.):*

- Stasera vengo **da** te, ma prima passo da Roberto.
  (I'm coming to your house tonight, but I'm going to stop off at Robert's before.)
- Sarò **dal** dentista alle 4 oggi pomeriggio.
  (I'll be at the dentist's at 4 o'clock this afternoon.)

When talking about shops you can use either the shop owner's profession or the kind of shop in question:

- Vado **dal** macellaio.   Or: – Vado **in** macelleria.
  (I'm going to the butcher's)

DA... A...   *(From........ to)*

- In treno si va **da** Milano **a** Bologna in due ore.
  (It takes two hours from Milano to Bologna by train.)

SU *(On)*

(Under) **SOTTO**

Il gatto è **sulla** sedia.
(The cat is on the chair.)

Il gatto è **sotto** la sedia.
(The cat is under the chair.)

FRA/TRA *(Among, between)*

(Behind) **DIETRO**

Il gatto dorme **tra** le sedie.
*(The cat is sleeping
between the two chairs.)*

Il gatto è **dietro** la sedia.
(The cat is behind the chair.)

DAVANTI A *(In front of)*   *(In, inside)* **DENTRO**

*Il gatto gioca **davanti**
allo specchio.*

*(The cat is playing
in front of the mirror.)*

*Il gatto dorme **dentro**
la scatola.*

*(The cat is sleeping
in/inside the box.)*

FUORI   *(Outside)*

*Il gatto dorme **fuori della** finestra.*

*(The cat is sleeping outside
the window.)*

ACCANTO A

(Next to)

*Il gatto è **accanto alla** finestra.*

(The cat is next to the window.)

PER/ATTRAVERSO

(Through, across)

*Mi piace camminare **per/attraverso** il centro di Roma.*
(I like walking through the centre of Roma.)

DI FIANCO A

(Beside/side by side)

*Il due gatti sono uno **di fianco all'**altro.*

(The two cats are side by side.)

FINO A

(Until, up to, as far as)

*Vada diritto **fino al** semaforo e poi volti a destra.*

(Go straight on until the traffic lights and and then turn right.)

LUNGO

(Along)

*Che bello camminare **lungo** i canali di Venezia.*

(Isn't it lovely walking along the canals in Venice.)

VICINO A *(Near/close to)*

LONTANO DA *(Far from)*

*Milano si trova **vicino a** Torino.*
(Milan is near Turin)

*Venezia si trova **lontano da** Palermo.*
(Venice is a long away from Palermo.)

SOPRA

(On, above, over)

*Il libro è **sopra** il tavolo.*

(The book is on the table.)

A *(At)*

IN *(In)*

● When talking about the time:

*Mi sveglio spesso **alle** 7.*
(I often wake up at 7.)

● With the months of the year:

*Sono nato **in** ottobre.*
(I was born in October.)

See Unità 17 for the time.

▶ Study the example.
  – *Sono nata **il** 20 dicembre 1971.*
    (I was born on the 20th of December 1971.)

When the full date is given a preposition is **not** required.

● With seasons:
  – **In** primavera è bello fare passeggiate in campagna.
    (In spring it's lovely going for walks in the country.)

● With years:
  – **Nel** 1995 il mese di maggio è stato molto brutto. Pioveva ogni giorno.
    (In 1995 the month of May was terrible. It rained every day.)

● With centuries:
  – Ippolito Nievo è vissuto **nel** XIX secolo.
    (Ippolito Nievo lived in the 19th century.)

➤ With the days of the week a preposition is **not** required:
  – Linuccio ha fatto un esame **mercoledì** 14 giugno 1995.
  (Linuccio did an exam on Wednesday 14th June 1995)

When talking about repeated events the definite article is used before the day of the week:
  – La domenica non si lavora. *(People don't work on Sundays.)*

● In is also used to express the time necessary to do something:

– Ho fatto i compiti **in** due ore. = ci ho messo due ore a fare i compiti.

  (I did my homework in two hours.   *it took me two hours to do my homework.)*

– Si va da Perugia ad Assisi **in** 20 minuti. = ci vogliono 20 minuti da Perugia ad Assisi.

  (You can go from Perugia to Assisi in 20 minutes.   *it takes 20 minutes from Perugia to Assisi.)*

PER (For)	**TRA/FRA** (In/within)
● *Per* is used to talk about the length of time:	● *Tra* or *fra* are used to indicate the period between the present moment of time and the beginning of a future event.

- *Vado in vacanza* **per** *due settimane.*
(I'm going on holiday for two weeks.)

- **Fra** *venti minuti devo tornare a lavorare*
(I have to go back to work in twenty minutes.)

● It is also used for special holiday periods:
  – **Per** Natale vorrei andare a sciare.
  (I'd like to go skiing for Christmas.)

time prepositions (2)

(da, di, fino a, ecc.) (since/for, in, until, etc.)

28

DA	*(Since/for)*

● **Da** is used to indicate the beginning of an action which is still happening in the present:

Costantino studia **dal** 1977. = Costantino ha cominciato a studiare nel 1977.

(Constantino has been studying since 1977. *Constantino began to study in 1977.)*

▶ N.B. In Italian the verb is used in the present indicative.

DI	*(In)*

● With parts of the day:
  – **Di** mattino è bello stare a letto.
  (It's nice staying in bed in the morning.)

DA... A... *(From... to)*	**FINO A** *(Until)*

● **Da... a** is used to indicate the length of time, specifying both the starting and finishing time:

● **Fino a** is used to indicate when an on-going action comes to an end:

- Ho dormito **dalle** 11 di ieri sera fino **all'**una di oggi pomeriggio.

(I slept from 11 o'clock last night until 1 o'clock this afternoon.)

- Ieri sera ho guardato la TV **fino alle** 2.30.

(I watched TV until 2.30 last night.)

PRIMA *(Before)*

– **Prima di** andare in vacanza,/**Prima delle** vacanze, Giorgio Rossi era molto depresso.
(Before going on holiday/Before his holiday, Giorgio Rossi was very depressed.)

▶ **Prima** is followed by the preposition **di**. If the word **prima** is followed by a verb, then usually the *infinitive* of the verb is used, but if the subject of the two sentences changes, then it is necessary to use *prima + che + subjunctive*. See Unità 70 and 89.

– **Prima che** Giovanna arrivi, Patrizia pulirà la casa.
(Before Giovanna arrives, Patrizia will clean the house.)

DURANTE *(During)*   **MENTRE** *(While)*

– **Durante** le vacanze Giorgio Rossi pensava al suo futuro.
(During his holiday Giorgio Rossi thought about his future.)
– **Mentre** era in vacanza, Giorgio Rossi pensava al suo futuro.
(While he was on holiday, Giorgio Rossi thought about his future.)

▶ **Durante** is followed by a noun. **Mentre** is followed by a complete sentence; the accompanying verb is never used in the infinitive form.

DOPO *(After)*

– **Dopo** le **vacanze**, **Dopo** essere tornato dalle vacanze, la vita di Giorgio Rossi è cambiata completamente.
(After his holiday,/After returning from his holiday, Giorgio Rossi's life changed completely.)

▶ If the word **dopo** is followed by a verb, then usually the *perfect infinitive* form of the verb is used, but if the subject of the two sentences changes, then it is necessary to use *dopo + che + indicative*. See Unità 88.

– **Dopo che** sua madre era arrivata, Paolo uscì a far la spesa.
(After his mother arrived, Paolo went out to do some shopping.)

prepositions (1)
(di, a, da, ecc.) (of/in/about, to, by, etc.)

29

■ In this unit a lot of terminology is used.
Don't worry about it too much!
Study the examples carefully and check with Appendix 3.

DI *(Of, about, than, by)*

– Questa è la casa **di** Mario. ⟶ *possession*
  (This is Mario's house.)
– Un disco **di** Luciano Pavarotti. ⟶ *author*
  (A record by Luciano Pavarotti.)
– Una lattina **di** birra. *(A can of beer.)* ⟶ *category*
– Una scultura di legno. ⟶ *material*
  (A wooden sculpture.)
– Un gatto **di** sette chili. ⟶ *size*
  (A cat weighing 7 kilos.)
– Un vecchio **di** 90 anni. ⟶ *age*
  (A 90-year old man).
– Silvia mi ha parlato **del** suo viaggio. ⟶ *topic*
  (Silvia told me about her trip.)
– Giovanni è più giovane **di** Marco. ⟶ *comparison*
  (Giovanni is younger than Marco.)
  (See Unità 59)

A *(To, at, with)*

– Ho dato l'invito **a** Giuseppe. ⟶ *indirect object*
  (I gave the invitation to Giuseppe.)
– Non sono mai salito su un treno **a** vapore. ⟶ *means*
  (I've never been on a steam train.)
– Nadia si è sposata **a** 25 anni. ⟶ *age*
  (Nadia got married at 25.)

– Una maglietta **a** righe.   ⟶ *kind*
  (A striped T-shirt.)
– Un piatto di spaghetti **al** burro e   ⟶ *flavour and*
  un gelato **al** limone.   *dish*
  *(A plate of spaghetti with butter, and a
  lemon flavoured ice-cream.)*

DA   *(From, out of, by)*

– Ho comprato un costume **da** bagno blu. ⟶ *purpose*
  (I've bought a blue swimming costume.)
– **Da** piccolo volevo fare il medico.   ⟶ *condition*
  (When I was young I wanted to be a doctor.)
– Una banconota **da** 10 euro.   ⟶ *amount*
  (A 10 euro banknote.)
– Ieri ho pianto **dalla** rabbia.   ⟶ *cause*
  (I was so angry I cried yesterday.)
– La Divina Commedia è stata scritta **da** Dante. ⟶ *agent*
  (The Divine Comedy was written by Dante.)

(See Unità 75).

▸ With **lontano** and **diverso** *(far from and different from/to)*

– Napoli è diversa **da** Milano.
  (Naples is different from Milan.)
– Palermo si trova lontano **da** Torino.
  (Palermo is far away from Turin.)

prepositions (2)

(in, con, su, ecc.) (by, with, about, etc.)

30

■ In this unit a lot of terminology is used. Don't worry about it too much!

Study the examples carefully and check with Appendix 3.

IN   *(By)*

– Vado spesso all'università **in** bicicletta.   ⟶   *means*
  (I often go to university by bike.)   *of transport*

CON   *(With)*

– Domani esco **con** Natalia.   ⟶   *company*
  (I'm going out with Natalia tomorrow.)
– Luigi parla **con** un forte accento siciliano. ⟶   *manner*
  (Luigi speaks with a strong Sicilian accent.)
– Un bimbo **con** i capelli ricci.   ⟶   *kind*
  (A boy with curly hair.)
– Mi piace bere un bicchiere di rum **con** ghiaccio. ⟶ *union*
  (I like drinking rum with ice.)

▶ **Senza** is the opposite of **con**
Mi piace bere il rum **senza** ghiaccio.
(I like drinking rum without ice.)

SU   *(About, on)*

– Ieri ho visto un film **su** Malcolm X.   ⟶   *topic*
  (Yesterday I saw a film about Malcolm X.)
– Sandra è ormai **sulla** trentina.   ⟶   *a rough estimate*
  (Sandra is about thirty now.)   *of age, prices*
                                           and quantity

30

PER *(In order to, for)*

– Bisogna lavorare **per** vivere   ⟶ *purpose*
(You need to work in order to live.)

– Ho comprato una macchina usata **per** 10.000 euro. ⟶ *price*
(I bought a second-hand car for 10.000 euro.)

– Ogni giovane deve studiare **per** il proprio futuro. ⟶ *advantage/*
(All young people have to study for their own future.) *disadvantage*

● With the following expressions:

per esempio,	*(for example)*
per caso,	*(by chance)*
per fortuna,	*(fortunately)*
per piacere/favore,	*(please)*
per telefono.	*(on the phone)*

FRA/TRA *(Among, between, out of)*

– **Fra** i libri che ho letto di recente "Los pasos ⟶ *partitive*
pedidos" è il più interessante.
(Out of all the books I've read recently
"Los pasos perdidos" is the most interesting.)

Study the picture.

- Oggi a pranzo **ho mangiato** un buon piatto di pesce.
(At lunch time today I ate a delicious plate of fish)

The **passato prossimo** is formed with the present indicative of *essere* or *avere* + the *past participle* of the main verb.

Many verbs have a regular form of the **past participle**.

-ARE	cantare (sing)	can**tato**
-ERE	credere (believe)	cred**uto**
-IRE	dormire (sleep)	dorm**ito**

Here is a list of the irregular **past participles** of many common verbs:

accendere (turn on)	acceso	mettere (put)	messo
aprire (open)	aperto	morire (die)	morto
bere (drink)	bevuto	muovere (move)	mosso
chiedere (ask)	chiesto	nascere (be born)	nato
chiudere (close)	chiuso	nascondere (hide)	nascosto
correggere (correct)	corretto	offrire (offer)	offerto
correre (run)	corso	perdere (lose)	perso (perduto)
cuocere (cook)	cotto	piacere (like)	piaciuto
decidere (decide)	deciso	piangere (cry)	pianto
dire (say/tell)	detto	porre (place)	posto
dividere (divide)	diviso	prendere (take)	preso
essere (be)	stato	ridere (laugh)	riso
fare (do/make)	fatto	rimanere (stay)	rimasto
leggere (read)	letto		

risolvere *(solve)*	risolto
rispondere *(answer)*	risposto
rompere *(break)*	rotto
scegliere *(choose)*	scelto
scrivere *(write)*	scritto
succedere *(happen)*	successo
togliere *(remove)*	tolto
tradurre *(translate)*	tradotto
uccidere *(kill)*	ucciso
vedere *(see)*	visto (veduto)
venire *(come)*	venuto
vincere *(win)*	vinto
vivere *(live)*	vissuto

■ Past participle agreements

● Study the following examples.
- Gloria **è** anda**ta** in discoteca sabato sera.
  (Gloria went to the disco on Saturday evening.)
- **Siamo** tornati dalle vacanze da poco e ora non abbiamo voglia di lavorare. *(We aren't long back from our holidays and now we don't feel like working.)*

When **essere** is used the *past participle* agrees with the *subject*, both in number (singular or plural) and gender (masculine or feminine).

● Osserva l'esempio: – Cinzia **ha** ordina**to** una birra gelata. *(Cinzia has ordered a really cold beer.)*

When **avere** is used there is usually no need for past participle agreement.

● When the *past participle* follows a *direct object* the agreement is optional:
- **Vi** hanno sentito/i cantare giovedì sera a teatro. *(They heard you all sing at the theatre on Thursday evening.)*

> *È un po' che non vedi Silvia e Cristina?*

> *Le ho viste ieri sera in piazza.*

➤ Exception: when the pronouns **lo, la, l', li, le,** are used with **avere**, then the agreement is necessary.

■ The **passato prossimo** is used to talk about actions related to present time.

● It is used to talk about actions that take place in an unfinished time period.

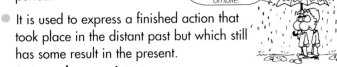

Questa settimana il tempo è stato orribile.

● It is used to express a finished action that took place in the distant past but which still has some result in the present.

– Ieri sera **ho mangiato** troppo e non **sono riuscito** a dormire tutta la notte! *(I ate too much yesterday evening and didn't manage to sleep all night.)*

▶ In Northern Italy, to talk about the past, the passato prossimo is preferred to the passato remoto in spoken language. The passato remoto is now used mainly for written Italian.

– Sette anni fa **sono andato** in Nicaragua.
(I went to Nicaragua seven years ago.)

■ When forming the **passato prossimo**, the auxiliary verb **essere** is used in the following cases:

● with **intransitive verbs**. These are verbs that do not have a direct object. (See Appendix 3).
The majority of these verbs fall into the following categories:

– **verbs indicating movement** ⟶ andare, arrivare, tornare, ecc. *(go, arrive, return, etc.)*

– **verbs indicating state** ⟶ stare, rimanere, ecc. *(be, stay, etc.)*

– **verbs indicating a change of state** ⟶ diventare, nascere, morire, ecc. *(become, be born, die, etc.)*

- **reflexive verbs**: – **Mi sono** appena **alzato** e sono già stanco. *(I have just got up and I'm tired already.)*

- ***essere*** is also used with other verbs:
  - **Sono bastati** dieci minuti per tornare a casa. ➤ bastare
    (I only needed 10 minutes to get home)   *(be enough/need)*
  - Mi è **piaciuta** molto la festa di sabato sera. ➤ piacere *(like)*
    (I really liked the party on Saturday evening.)

Essere is also used with the following common verbs: sembrare *(seem)*, parere *(seem/think)*, accadere/succedere *(happen)*, costare *(cost)*, mancare *(miss)*, dipendere *(depend)*, dispiacere *(displease/mind)*, toccare *(touch)*, occorrere *(to be necessary)*.

▶ See Unità 31, for the **subject** and **past participle** agreements.

◼ When forming the **passato prossimo**, the auxiliary verb **avere** is used in the following cases:

- with **transitive verb**. These are verbs which are followed by a direct object. (See Appendix 3):
  - Ieri **ho mangiato** le prime fragole della stagione.
    (Yesterday I ate the first strawberries of the season.)

With some verbs the auxiliary **avere** is required when the verb is used transitively, i.e. verb + direct object.
  - **Ho** cominciato il mio nuovo libro la settimana scorsa.
    (I started my new book last week.)
  - **Ho** finito il primo e ora prendo un piatto di carne ai ferri.
    (I've finished my first course and I'll have some grilled meat now.)

However, when such verbs are used intransitively, i.e. the verb is not followed by an object, then the auxiliary **essere** is used.

– Il film **è** cominciato mezz'ora fa.
 (The film started half an hour ago.)
– Il corso **è** finito in anticipo oggi.
 (The course finished early today.)

Here is a list of other verbs that can take either the auxiliary **essere** (when used intransitively) or **avere** (when used transitively): scendere *(go down/get off)*, salire *(go up/get on)*, passare *(go past)*, continuare *(continue)*, bruciare *(burn)*, saltare *(jump)*, cambiare *(change)*, aumentare *(increase)*, diminuire *(reduce, decrease)*.

■ Study the following examples:
– Ieri non **sono** potuto **andare** al mare, perché pioveva.
 (Yesterday I wasn't able to go to the seaside because it was raining.)
– **Ho** dovuto **mangiare** tutto, per non offendere il cuoco.
 (I had to eat everything, so as not to offend the cook.)

With the verbs **potere**, **volere**, and **dovere** the auxiliary required depends on the verb that follows.

▶ In spoken Italian the auxiliary verb **avere** is used more and more frequently regardless of the verb.

33

imperfect - form

(mangiavo, ecc.) (I ate, I was eating/I used to eat, etc.)

■ Regular verbs

I - ARE: cantare *(sing)*		II - ERE: vedere *(see)*	
(io)	cant **-avo**	(io)	ved **-evo**
(tu)	cant **-avi**	(tu)	ved **-evi**
(lui, lei)	cant **-ava**	(lui, lei)	ved **-eva**
(noi)	cant **-avamo**	(noi)	ved **-evamo**
(voi)	cant **-avate**	(voi)	ved **-evate**
(loro)	cant **-avano**	(loro)	ved **-evano**

III a - IRE: sentire *(hear)*		III b - IRE: finire *(finish)*	
(io)	sent **-ivo**	(io)	fin **-ivo**
(tu)	sent **-ivi**	(tu)	fin **-ivi**
(lui, lei)	sent **-iva**	(lui, lei)	fin **-iva**
(noi)	sent **-ivamo**	(noi)	fin **-ivamo**
(voi)	sent **-ivate**	(voi)	fin **-ivate**
(loro)	sent **-ivano**	(loro)	fin **-ivano**

■ The verbs *essere* and *avere*

avere *(have)*		essere *(be)*	
(io)	**avevo**	(io)	**ero**
(tu)	**avevi**	(tu)	**eri**
(lui, lei)	**aveva**	(lui, lei)	**era**
(noi)	**avevamo**	(noi)	**eravamo**
(voi)	**avevate**	(voi)	**eravate**
(loro)	**avevano**	(loro)	**erano**

■ Irregular verbs

dire *(say)*		fare *(do, make)*		porre *(put/place)*	
(io)	**dicevo**	(io)	**facevo**	(io)	**ponevo**
(tu)	**dicevi**	(tu)	**facevi**	(tu)	**ponevi**
(lui, lei)	**diceva**	(lui, lei)	**faceva**	(lui, lei)	**poneva**
(noi)	**dicevamo**	(noi)	**facevamo**	(noi)	**ponevamo**
(voi)	**dicevate**	(voi)	**facevate**	(voi)	**ponevate**
(loro)	**dicevano**	(loro)	**facevano**	(loro)	**ponevano**

tradurre *(translate)*		trarre *(pull, draw)*	
(io)	**traducevo**	(io)	**traevo**
(tu)	**traducevi**	(tu)	**traevi**
(lui, lei)	**traduceva**	(lui, lei)	**traeva**
(noi)	**traducevamo**	(noi)	**traevamo**
(voi)	**traducevate**	(voi)	**traevate**
(loro)	**traducevano**	(loro)	**traevano**

▶ Also: *bevevo*. *(I drank)*

■ When using the imperfect the main stress falls on the second syllable from the end, for example: io dic**e**vo, noi cantav**a**mo, voi erav**a**te, ecc. *(I said, we sang, you were, etc.)*

▶ The third person plural (**loro**) has the stress on the third vowel from the end, for example: loro dic**e**vano, cant**a**vano, **e**rano, ecc. *(they said, sang, were, etc.)*

34

imperfect - use

(mentre andavo a casa, ecc.) (while I was going home, etc.)

■ The **imperfect** is used in the following cases:

● Study the examples.

– Mentre **facevo**¹ colazione, è arrivata² (arrivò) mia madre.
(While I was having breakfast, my mother arrived.)

– **Studiavo**¹ all'Università di Firenze, quando scoppiò² (è scoppiata) la Seconda Guerra Mondiale.
(I was studying at Florence University, when the Second World War broke out.)

To talk about an on-going action in the past, "interrupted" by another event (the latter expressed with the **passato remoto** or **passato prossimo**).

● Study the examples.

– Quando **ero** piccolo, **andavo** spesso a giocare a calcio.
(When I was young, I often used to/would often go and play football.)

– D'estate mi **piaceva** leggere libri in giardino.
(In the summer I used to enjoy reading books in the garden.)

To talk about a habitual or repeated action in the past.

● Study the examples.

– Mentre lavoravamo, il cane ci guardava e scodinzolava.
(While we were working, the dog watched us and wagged his tails.)

– Federico **dormiva**, Laura **stirava** e nessuno **si preoccupava** del piccolo Alfredo, che **piangeva**.
(Federico was sleeping, Laura was ironing and no one was worried about little Alfredo, who was crying.)

To talk about two or more past actions taking place simultaneously in a past time period.

● For the use of the imperfect in a hypothetical clause, see Unità 74.
● For the use of the structure *stare* + gerund with the imperfect, see Unità 52.

■ Study the picture.

- Alessandro Manzoni **scrisse** i Promessi Sposi nel XIX secolo. *(Alessandro Manzoni wrote the Betrothed in the 19 th century.)*

■ **Regular verbs**

I - ARE: cantare *(sing)*		II - ERE: vendere *(sell)*	
(io)	cant **-ai**	(io)	vend **-ei** (**-etti**)
(tu)	cant **-asti**	(tu)	vend **-esti**
(lui, lei)	cant **-ò**	(lui, lei)	vend **-é** (**-ette**)
(noi)	cant **-ammo**	(noi)	vend **-emmo**
(voi)	cant **-aste**	(voi)	vend **-este**
(loro)	cant **-arono**	(loro)	vend **-erono** (**-ettero**)

III a - IRE: sentire *(hear)*		III b - IRE: finire *(finish)*	
(io)	sent **-ii**	(io)	fin **-ii**
(tu)	sent **-isti**	(tu)	fin **-isti**
(lui, lei)	sent **-ì**	(lui, lei)	fin **-ì**
(noi)	sent **-immo**	(noi)	fin **-immo**
(voi)	sent **-iste**	(voi)	fin **-iste**
(loro)	sent **-irono**	(loro)	fin **-irono**

▶ Even with the third person plural, the word stress is placed on the first vowel of the **passato remoto** ending.
For example: cant**a**rono, vend**e**ttero, sent**i**rono, etc.
(not cantar**o**no, etc.).

■ **Verbs *essere* and *avere***

avere		essere	
(io)	**ebbi**	(io)	**fui**
(tu)	**avesti**	(tu)	**fosti**
(lui, lei)	**ebbe**	(lui, lei)	**fu**
(noi)	**avemmo**	(noi)	**fummo**
(voi)	**aveste**	(voi)	**foste**
(loro)	**ebbero**	(loro)	**furono**

■ **Common irregular verbs**

bere *(drink)*	bevvi/bevetti	mettere *(put)*	misi
cadere *(fall)*	caddi	nascere *(be born)*	nacque
chiedere *(ask)*	chiesi	perdere *(lose)*	persi
conoscere *(know)*	conobbi	prendere *(take)*	presi
correre *(run)*	corsi	rendere *(return)*	resi
dare *(give)*	diedi (detti)	rispondere *(answer)*	risposi
decidere *(decide)*	decisi	rompere *(break)*	ruppi
fare *(make/do)*	feci	sapere *(know)*	seppi

scrivere *(write)*	scrissi
spegnere *(turn off)*	spensi
stare *(be, stay)*	stetti
tenere *(hold)*	tenni
vedere *(see)*	vidi
venire *(come)*	venni
vivere *(live)*	vissi
volere *(want)*	volli

▶ In most cases only **io, lui/lei, loro,** adopt the irregular
forms, while the other persons maintain the infinitive stem.

Io *ruppi*	noi rompemmo
tu rompesti	voi rompeste
lui *ruppe*	loro *ruppero*

■ The **passato remoto** is used to talk about an action
completely finished in the past.
   – Alla fine degli anni sessanta l'uomo **mise** piede sulla luna.
   (Man first walked on the moon at the end of the 60s.)

▶ In Northern and some central parts of Italy, the **passato
prossimo** is used in spoken language instead of the **passato
remoto** to express past actions. The **passato remoto** is now
mainly used in written Italian.
   – La prima volta che **sono andato** a Parigi avevo 17 anni.
   (The first time I went to Paris I was 17.)
   – La prima volta che **andai** a Parigi avevo 17 anni.
   (The first time I went to Paris I was 17.)

■ In Italian there are two aspects of the past: the **imperfect** and the **perfect** (*passato prossimo* and *passato remoto*).

The **imperfect** is used to talk about a finished action in the past, seen as if it were an on-going event, i.e. happening around a certain time: – Ieri alle 23,15 **guardavo** una partita alla televisione. *(I was watching a football match on television at 23.15 yesterday).*	The **passato prossimo** or **passato remoto** are used to talk about a finished action in the past, but not as if it were an on-going event: – **Ho vissuto** in Inghilterra per vari anni. *(I lived in England for several years.)* ▶ The duration of the action is not important: if the action is finished, then the **passato prossimo** or **passato remoto** is used. – La schiavitù in America **durò** diversi secoli. *(Slavery lasted for several centuries in America.)*
The **imperfect** is used to talk about an on-going action in the past, "interrupted" by another event: – Mentre **guardavo** la televisione, **è andata** via la corrente. *(While I was watching television, the electricity was cut off.)* – Quando **è arrivata** sua madre, Luca **dormiva**. *(When his mother arrived, Luca was sleeping.)* ▶ Note that **mentre** (*while*) is followed by the **imperfect**.	The **passato prossimo** or **passato remoto** are used to talk about an action that interrupts another on-going event in the past: – Quando **è arrivata** sua madre, Luca **dormiva**. *(When his mother arrived, Luca was sleeping.)* – Mentre **guardavo** la televisione, **è andata** via la corrente. *(While I was watching television, the electricity was cut off.)* ▶ Note that **quando** (*when*) is followed by the **passato prossimo** or **passato remoto**.

The **imperfect** is used to talk about simultaneous on-going actions in the past:	The **passato prossimo** or **passato remoto** are used to talk about finished actions which take place one after the other:
– Mentre lui **guardava** la TV, sua moglie **leggeva** un libro e il piccolo **dormiva**. *(While he was watching television, his wife was reading a book and the little one was sleeping.)*	– Ieri sera **ho guardato** una partita, poi **ho fatto** la doccia e **sono andato** a letto. *(Last night I watched a match, then I had a shower and went to bed.)*
The **imperfect** is used to talk about habitual or repeated actions in the past:	The **passato prossimo** or **passato remoto** are used to talk about one-off actions in the past, i.e. neither habitual or repeated events:
– Da piccolo mi **piaceva** andare al mare in estate, ma non **sopportavo** la montagna. *(When I was young I used to like going to the seaside in the summer, but I couldn't stand going to the mountains.)*	– Mi **è piaciuto** molto il viaggio in Giappone. *(I really enjoyed the trip to Japan.)*

future simple

(canterò, leggerò, ecc.)
(I will sing/I'm going to sing/I'm singing, etc.)

37

Regular verbs

I - ARE: cantare *(sing)*		II - ERE: credere *(believe)*	
(io)	cant -**erò**	(io)	cred -**erò**
(tu)	cant -**erai**	(tu)	cred -**erai**
(lui, lei)	cant -**erò**	(lui, lei)	cred -**erà**
(noi)	cant -**eremo**	(noi)	cred -**eremo**
(voi)	cant -**erete**	(voi)	cred -**erete**
(loro)	cant -**eranno**	(loro)	cred -**eranno**

III a - IRE: sentire *(hear)*		III b - IRE: finire *(finish)*	
(io)	sent -**irò**	(io)	fin -**irò**
(tu)	sent -**irai**	(tu)	fin -**irai**
(lui, lei)	sent -**irà**	(lui, lei)	fin -**irà**
(noi)	sent -**iremo**	(noi)	fin -**iremo**
(voi)	sent -**irete**	(voi)	fin -**irete**
(loro)	sent -**iranno**	(loro)	fin -**iranno**

▶ For the future the regular verbs belonging to group I change the **A** of the infinite -ARE into an **E**, for example: parl**e**rò (*I'll speak*), asp**e**tterò (*I'll wait*), etc.

Verbs *essere* and *avere*

avere		essere	
(io)	**avrò**	(io)	**sarò**
(tu)	**avrai**	(tu)	**sarai**
(lui, lei)	**avrà**	(lui, lei)	**sarà**
(noi)	**avremo**	(noi)	**saremo**
(voi)	**avrete**	(voi)	**sarete**
(loro)	**avranno**	(loro)	**saranno**

Irregular verbs

Verbs that drop the infinitive vowel.	andare (go)	andrò
	dovere (must)	dovrò
	potere (can)	potrò
	sapere (know)	saprò
	vedere (see)	vedrò
	vivere (live)	vivrò
Verbs that drop the infinitive vowel and change the **l** or the **n** of the stem into **rr**.	rimanere (stay)	rimarrò
	tenere (hold, keep)	terrò
	venire (come)	verrò
	volere (want)	vorrò
	bere (drink)	berrò
Verbs that maintain the infinitive **a**.	dare (give)	darò
	fare (do, make)	farò
	stare (be, stay)	starò

▶ With verbs ending in -**CARE** and -**GARE** an **H** is added before the **E**, for example:
spiegare (*explain*) ⟶ spiegherò, cercare (*look for*) ⟶ cercherò.
Verbs ending in -**CIARE** and -**GIARE** drop the **I**, for example:
annunciare (*announce*) ⟶ annuncerò, mangiare (*eat*) ⟶ mangerò.

■ The **future simple** is used:

● to talk about future events seen from the present:

*Fra due settimane **sarò** al caldo.*

● to talk about future uncertainty or doubts:
  – Che cosa **penseranno** di me i tuoi genitori?
  (What will your parents think of me?)

● **to express a supposition:**
  – **Sarai** stanco, ti porto a letto!
  (You must be tired, I'll take you to bed!)

▶ In Italian the **present indicative** is often used instead of the **future simple**:
  – Quest'estate **vado** in Turchia. *(This summer I'm going to Turkey.)*

■ Do you remember what a personal pronoun is? See Appendix 3.

■ **Subject pronouns**

	singular	plural
first person	io	noi
second person	tu	voi
third person	egli, lui, esso ella, lei, essa	essi, esse, loro

■ The subject pronoun is not often used in Italian:
  – Ho chiamato Carlo e gli ho detto della nuova casa.
  (I called Carlo and told him about the new house.)

However, in some cases it is necessary.

● When the speaker wants to contrast the two subjects in question:
  – **Lui** sa l'inglese, ma **lei** non capisce nemmeno una parola.
  (He speaks English but she doesn't understand a word.)

● When the speaker wants to emphasise the subject; in such
  cases the subject pronouns is often placed after the main verb;
  – Me l'ha detto **lei**, ma non ci credo.
  (She told me but I don't believe it.)

● When **anche, neanche, neppure, nemmeno** (*also, neither*)
  are used.
  – **Anche noi** vogliamo provare a giocare a squash.
  (We want to try to play squash, too.)

■ In modern Italian **lui** and **lei** are used much more than **egli,
ella, essa**. In the plural form **loro** takes the place of **essi** and
esse.
Esso is used for things or animals.

■ In Italian the subject pronoun **tu** is used when there is an *informal* relationship between the two speakers.
When the relationship is more *formal* then the polite form **lei** is used.

► Study the picture.

Lei (the polite form) is used for both masculine and feminine genders. It is sometimes written with a capital letter (**Lei**).

● In modern Italian the plural subject pronoun **voi** is almost always used for both polite and informal situations.

► The subject pronoun **Loro** is rarely used nowadays for the plural polite form.

(me, a te, ecc.) (me, to you, etc.)

■ Do you understand what is meant by "subject" and "object"?
See Appendix 3.

Object pronouns have both stressed and unstressed forms. If you
want to know why, see Appendix 3. Otherwise you need only
learn which are which.

■ **Object pronouns**

Stressed forms

	singular	plural
first person	**me** *(me)*	**noi** *(us)*
second person	**te** *(you)*	**voi** *(you)*
third person masculine	**lui, (esso)** *(him, it)*	**loro, (essi)** *(them)*
feminine	**lei, (essa)** *(her, it)*	**loro, (esse)** *(them)*
reflexive	**sé** *(oneself, etc.)*	**sé** *(themselves)*

Lui, lei, loro are used for people; **esso, essa, essi, esse** for both
things or people.

■ **Stressed object pronouns** are used:

● when preceded by a preposition, i.e. as **indirect object
pronouns**:

Posso venire **con te** *al mare domani?*

● to emphasise a person expressed with the object pronoun in
the sentence:
 – Hai visto **me** o mio fratello ieri al supermercato?
 (Did you see me or my brother at the supermarket yesterday?)

■ Study the example.

– **Prima di te** ho avuto colleghi insopportabili.
(The colleagues I had before you were unbearable.)

The stressed object pronouns are usually preceded by **di** when used with prepositions such as: *dentro, fuori, prima, dopo, sopra, sotto, senza, contro.*

■ **Sé** is the **reflexive** form for the third person singular and plural.

Sé can be made more emphatic by **se stesso/a/i/e**.
Note that with the form **se stesso** there is no accent on **sé**.

– Lui pensa solo a **sé** (**se stesso**) e non si interessa mai agli altri.
(He only thinks about himself and never takes other people into consideration.)

■ Can you remember the difference between a direct and indirect object pronoun? See Appendix 3.

■ Unstressed object pronouns are the most common. They are used as direct and indirect object pronouns when there is no need to give special emphasis to the pronoun.

Unstressed direct object pronouns

		singular	plural
first person		**mi** (me)	**ci** (us)
second person		**ti** (you)	**vi** (you)
third person	masculine	**lo/l'** (him, it)	**li** (them)
	feminine	**la/l'** (her, it)	**le** (them)
	reflexive	**si** (oneself, etc.)	**si** (themselves)

■ Unstressed pronouns are used as the direct object in a sentence. The direct object pronoun answers the question **chi?** and **che cosa?**

– Claudio, **ti** ho chiamato ieri, ma non eri in casa.
 (**Ti** = the person who was called, i.e.Claudio).
 (Claudio, I called you yesterday but you weren't at home.)

> – Quanti anni ha tua madre?
> – *How old's your mother?*
> – Non **lo** ricordo. – *I don't remember.*
> **Lo** is used to sunstitute a complete sentence.

■ **Unstressed indirect object pronouns**

		singular	plural
first person		**mi** (me)	**ci** (us)
second person		**ti** (you)	**vi** (you)
third person	masculine	**gli** (him, it)	**loro/gli** (them)
	feminine	**le** (her, it)	**loro/gli** (them)
	reflexive	**si** (oneself, etc.)	**si** (themselves)

■ Unstressed pronouns are used as the indirect object pronoun in a sentence, where the preposition is not expressed.

40

The indirect object pronoun answers the questions: **a chi? a che cosa?**
- Ho visto Silvio e **gli** ho detto di telefonare a Luca.
  (**Gli** = the person who was told to phone Luca, i.e. Silvio).
  (I saw Silvio and told him to telephone Luca.)

▶ The masculine and feminine form of the third person plural for the indirect object pronoun is **loro**. However, in modern Italian **gli** is often used instead of **loro** again for both sexes:
- I miei genitori mi hanno chiesto **quando** penso di sposarmi. Ho risposto **loro** che non lo sapevo/**Gli** ho risposto che non lo sapevo. *(My parents asked **when** I was thinking of getting married. I told them that I didn't know.)*

■ Unstressed object pronouns are placed.

● **before** the verb, when used in an indicative, conditional or subjunctive sentence:
- **Mi** dai un bicchiere d'acqua, per favore?
  (Can you give me a glass of water, please?)
- **Ti** piacerebbe, andare in vacanza in Madagascar?
  (Would you like to go to Madagascar on holiday?)
- Signora, **mi** dica, come fa a mantenersi così in forma?
  (Tell me, how do you manage to keep so fit?)

● **after** the verb, when used with an infinitive, a participle, a gerund or imperative. (II person singular and plural).
- Sarebbe bello conoscer**la** meglio, ma ha un marito molto geloso.
  (It would be nice to get to know her more, but her husband is very jealous.)
- Silvana ha accettato il contratto di lavoro proposto**le**.
  (Silvana accepted the contract they proposed.)
- Parlando**gli**, forse potrei capire il suo punto di vista.
  (Talking to him, maybe I could understand his point of view.)
- Lascia**mi** in piace, ti prego, non vedi che sto lavorando!
  (Leave me alone, can't you see I'm working!)

▶ When the infinitive is used with an unstressed pronoun the final **e** of the verb is dropped.
parlar**e** + **gli** ⟶ parlar**gli** *(Speak to him)*
legger**e** + **lo** ⟶ legger**lo** *(Read it)*

▶ With *dovere, potere, sapere* and *volere* two constructions are possible:
Voglio conoscer**la** or **La** voglio conoscere *(I want to meet her.)*

■ Look at the picture.

*A che ora **ti** sei alzato stamattina? Perché non **ti** sei lavato?*

■ **Alzarsi** and **lavarsi** are both reflexive verbs. Study the table below.

(io)	**mi** *(myself)*	lavo
(tu)	**ti** *(yourself)*	lavi
(lui, lei)	**si** *(himself, herself)*	lava
(noi)	**ci** *(ourselves)*	laviamo
(voi)	**vi** *(yourselves)*	lavate
(loro)	**si** *(themselves)*	lavano

■ Reflexive verbs consist of a reflexive pronoun together with the verb.

■ With compound tenses reflexive verbs always use the auxiliary verb **essere**.

__Mi sono__ svegliato tardi questa mattina e ho perso il treno.

For the past participle agreements with the verb **essere**, see Unità 31.

41

■ Some common reflexive verbs.

addormentarsi *(fall asleep)*	fidarsi *(trust)*
alzarsi *(get up)*	incontrarsi *(meet each other)*
ammalarsi *(take ill)*	lavarsi *(get washed)*
arrabbiarsi *(get angry)*	pettinarsi *(comb one's hair)*
bagnarsi *(get wet)*	riposarsi *(rest)*
chiamarsi *(be called)*	rompersi *(break)*
fermarsi *(stop)*	sedersi *(sit down)*

■ Some transitive verbs (see Appendix 3) become reflexive in order to emphasise meaning:
  – Ieri sera **mi sono** mangiato una pizza favolosa e **mi sono** bevuto una birra alla spina squisita!
   (Yesterday evening I devoured a wonderful pizza and downed some excellent beer!)
  – Ieri sera **ho** mangiato una pizza favolosa e **ho** bevuto una birra alla spina squisita!
   (Yesterday evening I ate a wonderful pizza and drank some excellent beer!)

■ The position of the reflexive pronouns follows the rules of the unstressed object pronouns. See Unità 40.

ci and *ne*
(ci vado domani, ne parlerò bene)
(I'm going there tomorrow, I'll speak well about it)

42

■ **Ci** is used

● with the meaning of **qui**, **lì** (*here, there*) in order to substitute a noun of place determining state or movement:

– Sei mai stata a Roma? - Sì, **ci** sono andata due anni fa.
(Have you ever been to Rome? - Yes, I went there two years ago.)

▶ Study the example.

– Oggi **a scuola** c'erano due studenti nuovi.
(There were two new students at school today.)

● With verbs that take the prepositions **a** *(pensare a)* (*think about*), **su** *(contare su)* (*count on*), to mean **a/su questo/ciò**, **a/su lui/lei/loro** (*about this/it, etc.*).

– Hai pensato **al** regalo per Roberto? - **Ci** ho pensato, ma non mi è venuto in mente niente.
(Did you think about a present for Roberto? - Yes, I did think about it, but nothing came to mind.)

– Posso contare **sulla** tua presenza al congresso?
  - Sì, **ci** puoi contare.
(Can I count on your presence at the congress? - Yes, you can count on it.)

■ **Vi** can be used instead of **ci**, but mainly in written language.

– È gradita la Sua presenza al ricevimento. La preghiamo di portar**vi** altra persona di suo gradimento.
(You are warmly invited to the reception. You are welcome to bring other guests of your choice.)

■ Sometimes in spoken language, **ci** is used without any particular meaning; for example with the verb **avere**, especially where the answer to a question contains the pronouns (**lo, la, l', li, le**).

– Hai ancora la tua mazza da baseball? - No, non **ce l'**ho più.
(Have you still got your baseball bat? - No, I haven't got it any more.)

See Unità 44: **ci** + pronouns.

■ **Ne** is used

● to replace an object noun or a whole sentence introduced by **di** or **da**, to give the meaning of di/da questo/a **di/da lui/lei/loro, da questo luogo**.

– Ti ricordi **di** Elsa? – Sì, me **ne** ricordo bene.
(Do you remember Elsa? - Yes, I remember her well.)

▶ – Chi mi ha detto che tornerai in Germania presto? Ah, sì, me **ne** ha parlato Gianni.
(Who told me you would go back to Germany soon? Ah, yes, Gianni told me about it.)

– Sono stato a Perugia, ne sono appena tornato.
(I've been to Perugia, I've just got back.)

When there is a compound tense, the past participle does not agree with the object introduced by **di**.

– Avete parlato **di** musica ieri sera? No, non **ne** abbiamo parla**to**.
(Did you talk about music yesterday evening? No, we didn't talk about it.)

■ Study the pictures.

> Quante **sigarette** fumi ogni giorno?

> **Ne** fumo cinquanta.

> Vuoi un bicchiere di **vino**?

> No, **ne** ho già bevuto troppo.

1

2

Ne is used to indicate **part** of a quantity and substitute a noun.
In example number 1, **ne** replaces the word "**sigarette**".
In the second example **ne** substitutes the word "**vino**".

> Hai fatto i compiti?

> Sì, **li** ho fatti **tutti.**

> Ci sono ancora delle sigarette nel pacchetto?

> Mi spiace, **le** ho fumate **tutte**.

3

4

In the first two examples only **part** of the quantity is expressed, in examples 3 and 4 the whole quantity is being expressed.
When the whole quantity is expressed, i.e. **tutto**, then the pronouns **lo/la/li/le** are used instead of **ne**.

● When the concept expresses **zero** quantity, i.e. **niente** or **nessuno**, then **ne** is used.
  – Quanti film di Fellini hai visto? – Non **ne** ho visto **nessuno**.
    (How many of Fellini's films have you seen? - I haven't seen any of them.)
  – Quanto latte bevi ogni giorno? – Non **ne** bevo.
    (How much milk do you drink a day? - I don't drink any.)

- In compound tenses, even with the auxiliary *avere*, the past participle agrees with the noun replaced by **ne**.
    - Quanti libri hai letto quest'estate? – **Ne** ho letti cinque.
      (How many books have you read this summer? - I've read five.)
    - Che dischi avete ascoltato alla festa? – **Ne** abbiamo ascoltati alcuni latino-americani molto belli.
      (Which records did you listen to at the party? - We listened to some really nice Latin American ones.)
    - Quanti turisti arriveranno quest'anno in Italia? – Non si sa, ma finora **ne** sono arrivati due milioni.
      (How many tourists will come to Italy this year? - It's not certain, but so far two million.)

▶ When the quantity expressed is zero (*nessuno, niente*), the past participle agrees only in gender and not in number.
    - Hai visto **le ragazze** del corso d'italiano?
      - No, non **ne** ho ancora vista **nessuna**.
        (Have you seen the girls on the Italian course?
      - *No, I haven't seen anyone yet.)*

- **Ne** is also used in specific expressions.
    - Non **ne** posso più, sono stanchissimo.
      (I can't take anymore, I'm really tired.)
    - Non voglio più vivere in Italia, me **ne** vado, torno in Germania. *(I don't want to live in Italy anymore. I'm leaving here and going back to Germany.)*
    - Ho detto a Martino la verità e se **n'**è avuto a male.
      (I told Martino the truth and he was really upset.)

		indirect							
		mi	*ti*	*gli/le*	*si*	*ci*	*vi*	*gli*	*si*
direct	*lo*	me lo	te lo	glielo	se lo	ce lo	ve lo	glielo	se lo
	la	me la	te la	gliela	se la	ce la	ve la	gliela	se la
	li	me li	te li	glieli	se li	ce li	ve li	glieli	se li
	le	me le	te le	gliele	se le	ce le	ve le	gliele	se le
	ne	me ne	te ne	gliene	se ne	ce ne	ve ne	gliene	se ne

● The *i* of **mi/ti/ci/vi/si** changes into an *e*, before another pronoun: **me lo**, etc.

● With combined pronouns the indirect object pronoun is placed before the direct object pronoun:
  – Chi ti ha dato quella bambola? - **Me l'**ha data la zia.
    (Who gave you that doll? - Aunty gave it to me.)

● Combined pronouns are written as two separate words, apart from the third person singular and plural **glielo**, etc.:
  – Devi consegnare il libro a Renato.
  – **Gliel'**ho già spedito, **me lo** ha richiesto ieri per telefono.
    (You have to get the book to Renato. - I've already sent it off to him, he asked me for it yesterday on the phone.)

● When the pronouns follow a verb in the form of the *infinitive*, *gerund*, *imperative* or as a *participle*, they are joined to the actual verb:
  – **Diteglielo** voi a Sandro; io gliel'ho già ripetuto tre volte!
    (You tell Sandro; I've already repeated it to him three times.)

▶ With the infinitive the verb drops the final **e**:
  – Stasera c'è la prima dell'Aida! Te ne sei dimenticato?
  - No, ma hai fatto bene a ricorda**rmelo**.
   *(It's the première of Aida this evening! Had you
   forgotten about it?
   No, but you did well to remind me.)*

● For the third person plural **gli** is commonly used nowadays.
  If **loro** is used, the sentence construction must be changed: the
  direct object pronoun **lo/la**/etc., is placed before the verb
  whereas the *indirect* object pronoun **loro** comes after the verb:
  – Hai detto ai tuoi genitori che hai una ragazza nuova?
                      – No, non **gliel**'ho ancora detto.
         Oppure: – No, non **l**'ho ancora detto **loro**.
  *(Have you told your parents that you've got a new girlfriend?
  No, I haven't told them yet.)*

■ **Pronouns +** *Ci* **(place)**

direct object pronouns	mi	ti	lo	la	ci	vi
	mi ci	ti ci	ce lo	ce la	no combination	vi ci

direct object pronouns	li	le	si	ne
	ce li	ce le	**ci si**	ce ne

  – Sei mai stato al Parco Ducale? – No, **mi ci** porti tu?
   *(Have you ever been to Parco Ducale? - No, will you take
   me there?)*

with no preposition	with a preposition
che	cui

■ **Che** and **cui** are *invariable* and are not used with an *article* (apart from the two cases below marked with *).

■ **Che** is *not* used with a preposition:
  – Gli amici **che** abbiamo visto ieri sera sono simpatici.
    (The friends (that) we saw yesterday evening are nice.)
  – Uno scrittore è una persona **che** scrive libri.
    (A writer is a person who writes books.)

■ **Cui** is used with a preposition:
  – Il film **di cui** ti ho parlato è stato girato in Italia.
    (The film (that) I spoke to you about was shot in Italy.)
  – La ragazza **con cui** sono andato in vacanza è partita per Londra.
    (The girl (who) I went on holiday with has left for London.)

■ When followed by **cui** the preposition **a** can be left out:
  – La ditta **(a) cui** ho scritto ha sede in Svizzera.
    (The firm (that) I wrote to is located in Switzerland.)
  – Il professore **(a) cui** hai parlato è molto disponibile.
    (The professor (that) you spoke to is very helpful.)

■ * When **cui** is placed between the definite article and the noun it expresses possession (whose):

– Il giovane, **il cui padre** lavora alla Fiat, sta facendo una
  ricerca sulla storia dell'automobile.
  *(The young man, whose father works for Fiat, is doing some
  research on the history of the car.)*

– Il pittore, **sulla cui arte** tanto si discute, è venezuelano.
  (The painter, whose art is so controversial, is Venezuelan.)

The article required depends on the noun which it refers to.

■ * **Il che** means *e questo /e ciò (which, this, that, it, etc.):*
  – Ieri mi ha telefonato Carla; **il che** *(e questo/e ciò)* mi ha
    fatto molto piacere.
    (Carla telephoned me yesterday, which made me very happy.)

■ **Chi** means *le persone che, quelli che, ecc. (the people
  who, those who, etc.):*

The verbs is always used in the third person singular:
  – **Chi** non lavora non mangia. *(If you don't work, you don't eat.)*
  – Parlo solo con **chi** sa ascoltare.
    (I only speak to those who know how to listen.)
  – **Chi** vuole frequentare il corso d'italiano deve iscriversi entro
    domani.
    *(Whoever wishes to attend the Italian course must enrol by
    tomorrow.)*

See Unità 19 for the interrogative **chi** (question word).

relative pronouns (2)

(il quale, della quale, ecc.) (who, of which, etc.)

46

■ Study the picture.

*Quella è la montagna **sulla quale** dobbiamo salire.*

■ *Relative pronouns* may also be expressed with **quale/i.**
This form is more frequent in the written language.

	singular	plural
masculine	il quale	i quali
feminine	la quale	le quali

– Quelle sono le ragazze con **le quali** siamo andati al mare.
  (Those are the girls (who) we went to the seaside with.)

These structures are variable and always require the definite
article. They agree with the word they refer to in both gender
and number.

■ With the prepositions **di, a, su, in,** compound forms of the
prepositions with the definite article are formed; see Unità 23:

– Ho visto nuovamente gli studenti **ai quali** ho dovuto dare un
  cattivo voto.
  (I saw the students once again who I gave bad marks to.)

▶ It is sometimes necessary to use the structures with **quale/i** to
avoid ambiguity.

Study the following example.

– Ieri ho visto Giovanni e sua nonna, **che** aveva appena
  comprato il pane.
  *(Yesterday I saw Giovanni and his grandmother, who had
  just bought some bread.)*

The use of **che** in this case creates ambiguity. It is better to say:

– Ieri ho visto Giovanni e sua nonna, **la quale** aveva appena
  comprato il pane.
  *(Yesterday I saw Giovanni and his grandmother who had
  just bought some bread.)*

Del quale expressing possession has the same construction as
other prepositional phrases:

– Questo è il giovane, i genitori **del quale** lavorano con me.
  (This is the young man whose parents work with me.)

Notice the different construction with **i cui**:

– Questo è il giovane, **i cui** genitori lavorano con me.
  (This is the young man whose parents work with me.)

▶ **Il quale** cannot be used as a direct object:

– Il ragazzo **che ho** conosciuto è giapponese.

~~il quale~~

(The boy (that) I met is Japanese.)

(avrò mangiato, sarai andato)
(I will have eaten, you will have gone)

sarò sarai sarà	partito/a	avrò avrai avrà	mangiato
saremo sarete saranno	partiti/e	avremo avrete avranno	mangiato

■ The **future perfect** is formed with the *future simple* of the auxiliaries *essere* or *avere* and the *past participle* of the verb.

■ Study the examples.

```
2003              2005                          2006
 |*                *|                            *|
 |--------------------|----------------------------|
 |                    |                            |
```

Oggi dipendo dai miei genitori, ma **dopo che** mi **sarò laureato**, cercherò un lavoro.
(Now I'm dependant on my parents but after gratuating I will look for a job.)

```
ore 20.00                        ore 20.10
 |*                                *|
 |----------------------------------|
 |                                  |
```

Quando avrò finito di mangiare, farò una doccia.
(When I have finished eating, I will have a shower.)

The **future perfect** expresses a future action which takes place before another relevant action in the future and is often introduced by **dopo che** or **quando**.

● It is also used to express **uncertainty** or **doubt** referring to the past:

*Che cosa **avranno pensato** di me i tuoi genitori, quando mi hanno visto?*

● to express a **supposition** referring to the past:

– **Sarai stato** stanco ieri sera, dopo 4 ore in discoteca!
(You must have been tired last night after 4 hours in a disco!)

■

| ero
eri
era | partito/a | avevo
avevi
aveva | mangiato |
| eravamo
eravate
erano | partiti/e | avevamo
avevate
avevano | mangiato |

■ The **past perfect** is formed with the *imperfect* of the auxiliaries *essere* or *avere* and the *past participle* of the verb.

■ The **past perfect** is used to talk about an action which takes place *before* another event in the past expressed with the **passato prossimo/passato remoto** or **imperfect**:

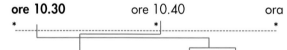

ore 10.30   ore 10.40   ora

– Il treno per Londra delle 10.30 **era** già **partito**, quando Giorgio **arrivò** alla stazione.
(The 10.30 train to London had already left when Giorgio got to the station.)

When the **past perfect** is used with an *imperfect,* there is often a reference to repeated or habitual actions in the past:

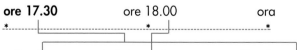

ore 17.30   ore 18.00   ora

– Ogni sera quando Luisa **arrivava** a casa, Claudio **aveva** già **preparato** da mangiare.
(When Luisa got home every evening, Claudio had already prepared the meal.)

ore 19.30   **ore 20.10**   ora
* - *- - - - - - - - - - - - - -*

– Dato che **aveva finito** di lavorare tardi, Silvia non **riuscì** ad andare al cinema.
   (As she was late in finishing work, Silvia wasn't able to go to the cinema.)

■ Study the two previous examples.
   Is the **past perfect** only used in main clauses?

It can be used both in the main clause and in subordinate clauses.

► See Unità 80 - The trapassato remoto.

Regular verbs

I - ARE: cantare *(sing)*	II - ERE: credere *(believe)*
(io) cant **-erei**	(io) cred **-erei**
(tu) cant **-eresti**	(tu) cred **-eresti**
(lui, lei) cant **-erebbe**	(lui, lei) cred **-erebbe**
(noi) cant **-eremmo**	(noi) cred **-eremmo**
(voi) cant **-ereste**	(voi) cred **-ereste**
(loro) cant **-erebbero**	(loro) cred **-erebbero**

III a - IRE: sentire *(hear)*	III b - IRE: finire *(finish)*
(io) sent **-irei**	(io) fin **-irò**
(tu) sent **-iresti**	(tu) fin **-iresti**
(lui, lei) sent **-irebbe**	(lui, lei) fin **-irebbe**
(noi) sent **-iremmo**	(noi) fin **-iremmo**
(voi) sent **-ireste**	(voi) fin **-ireste**
(loro) sent **-irebbero**	(loro) fin **-irebbero**

▶ The conditional of regular and irregular verbs is formed in the same way as the future simple but with different endings.

Verbi *essere* e *avere*

avere		essere	
(io)	**avrei**	(io)	**sarei**
(tu)	**avresti**	(tu)	**saresti**
(lui, lei)	**avrebbe**	(lui, lei)	**sarebbe**
(noi)	**avremmo**	(noi)	**saremmo**
(voi)	**avreste**	(voi)	**sareste**
(loro)	**avrebbero**	(loro)	**sarebbero**

■ Irregular verbs

Verbs that drop the infinitive vowel.	and**a**re *(go)* do**ve**re *(must, have to)* po**te**re *(can, be able to)* sa**pe**re *(know)* ve**de**re *(see)* vi**ve**re *(live)*	an**drei** do**vrei** po**trei** sa**prei** ve**drei** vi**vrei**
Verbs that drop the infinitive vowel and change the l or the n of the stem into rr.	rima**ne**re *(stay)* te**ne**re *(keep)* ve**ni**re *(come)* vo**le**re *(want)* be**re** *(drink)*	rima**rrei** te**rrei** ve**rrei** vo**rrei** be**rrei**
Verbs that mantain the infinitive a.	d**a**re *(give)* f**a**re *(do, make)* st**a**re *(stay)*	d**arei** f**arei** st**arei**

▶ With verbs ending in -**CARE** and -**GARE** an **H** is added before the **E**, e.g.:

spie**gare** ⟶	spie**gherei**	*(explain)*
cer**care** ⟶	cer**cherei**	*(look for)*

Verbs ending in -**CIARE** and -**GIARE** drop the **I**, e.g.:

annun**ciare** ⟶	annun**cerei**	*(announce)*
man**giare** ⟶	man**gerei**	*(eat)*

conditional - use

(mangeresti una mela?, ecc.) (would you eat an apple?, etc.)

50

■ The **conditional** is used in a *present* or *future* time period to express something more politely, i.e.:

● a **request**:
  – Mi **daresti** il numero di tua sorella, per favore?
  (Would you give me your sister's phone number, please?)

● a **wish**:
  – **Vorrei** tanto andare in vacanza!
  (I would love to go on holiday!)

In the two examples above do the actions take place in the present, the future or the past?
It is important to understand this in order to use the conditional correctly.

With a present or future time reference, it is also used to express:

● a **doubt**:
  – Non so se Giovanni **verrebbe** a cena da noi domani sera.
  (I don't know if Giovanni would come to dinner at our place tomorrow evening.)

● a **personal opinion**:
  – A mio parere il governo **dovrebbe** fare di più per combattere la disoccupazione.
  (In my opinion the Government should do more to fight unemployment.)

● to report **unconfirmed news**:
  – Il Primo Ministro inglese **arriverebbe** in Italia il mese prossimo.
  (The English Prime Ministre should arrive in Italy next month)

● to politely express **orders**, **strong suggestions** or **advice**, often with the conditional of the verb dovere:
  – Ragazzi, **dovreste** studiare di più!*(You should study more, kids!)*
  – Sig. Santi, Lei **dovrebbe** smettere di fumare.
  (Mr Santi, you ought to give up smoking.)

▶ For the use of **vorrei**, see Unità 14.
For the use of the **conditional** in *hypothetical clauses*, see Unità 74.

51

perfect conditional
(avrei mangiato, saresti andato)
(I would have eaten, you would have gone)

■ Study the following example.
Does it refer to the present or the past?

– L'anno scorso **mi sarebbe piaciuto** andare alla Fiera di Francoforte.
(I would have liked to go to the fair in Frankfurt last year.)

■

sarei saresti sarebbe	partito/a	avrei avresti avrebbe	mangiato
saremmo sareste sarebbero	partiti/e	avremmo avreste avrebbero	mangiato

■ The **perfect conditional** is formed with the *conditional* of the auxiliaries *essere* or *avere* and the *past participle* of the verb.

■ The **perfect conditional** is used to express the following in the *past*:

● an unfulfilled **wish**:
– **Sarei andato** volentieri al mare domenica scorsa, ma purtroppo pioveva.
(I would have loved to go to the sea last Sunday, but unfortunately it was raining.)

● some **unconfirmed news**:
– Secondo voci non ancora confermate, il terremoto **avrebbe causato** danni per oltre mille miliardi.
(According to unconfirmed reports the earthquake may have caused over 1,000 billion worth of damage.)

■ The **perfect conditional** is also used as **future in the past**, i.e. it is used to talk about an action which takes place in a future time with respect to a past action:

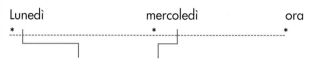

Lunedì   mercoledì   ora

– Gregorio **disse** che **sarebbe arrivato** mercoledì.
(Gregorio said he would arrive on Wednesday.)

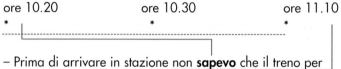

ore 10.20   ore 10.30   ore 11.10

– Prima di arrivare in stazione non **sapevo** che il treno per Londra delle 10.30 **sarebbe partito** con 40 minuti di ritardo.
(Before getting to the station I didn't know the 10.30 train to London would be delayed 40 minutes.)

■ For the use of the **perfect conditional** in *hypothetical clauses*, see Unità 74.

■ Study the picture.

■ The structure **stare + gerund**
indicates an on-going action:
- Le vacanze **stanno
  trascorrendo** senza incidenti.
  (The holidays are going well.)

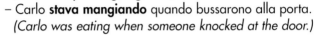

*Sta piovendo di
nuovo, non è possibile!*

- Carlo **stava mangiando** quando bussarono alla porta.
  (Carlo was eating when someone knocked at the door.)

■ The structure s**tare + gerund** is used almost exclusively with
the *present* and the *imperfect* forms, occasionally with the
future simple, but **never** with compound tenses (passato
prossimo, trapassati, future perfect, etc.):
- Ieri ~~sono stato dormendo~~ tutto il pomeriggio.
- Ieri **ho dormito** tutto il pomeriggio. *(I slept all afternoon yesterday.)*

■ It is not necessary to use the structure **stare + gerund**.
The present or imperfect are often used in its place:
- **Nevica** da questa mattina.
- **Sta nevicando** da questa mattina.
  (It has been snowing since this morning.)

■ The structure **stare + gerund** is used almost exclusively with
verbs which express an action, but it is generally not used
with verbs of feeling or opinion; *essere; avere; dovere;
volere; potere; sapere; stare (be, have, must/have to, want,
can/be able to, know, stay)*, etc.
- Il bambino **stava giocando** con il suo gatto, quando
  arrivarono i genitori.
  (The little boy was playing with his cat when his parents arrived.)
- ~~Sto sapendo~~ che Luisa torna il 30 agosto dalla montagna.
- **So** che Luisa torna il 30 agosto dalla montagna.
  *(I know that Luisa is coming back from the mountains on
  30th August.)*

For the gerund, see Unità 90.

■ Study the picture.

> Sbrighiamoci a tornare a casa, **sta per piovere!**

■ The structure **stare per + infinitive** indicates an *imminent* action:

– **Stavo per fermarmi** al semaforo, quando un'auto mi ha tamponato.

(I was about to stop at the traffic lights when a car ran into the back of me.)

■ The structure **stare + infinitive** is used almost exclusively with the *present* and *imperfect* forms, occasionally with the future simple, but **never** with compound tenses (passato prossimo, trapassati, future perfect, etc.). See Unità 52.

– Il bambino **stava per uscire**, quando sua mamma lo ha chiamato.

(The little boy was about to go out when his Mum called him.)

– Mia sorella **sta per tornare** dalla Gran Bretagna.

(My sister will soon be coming back from Great Britain.)

54

■ There are:
  - *indefinite adjectives only*
  - *indefinite adjectives and pronouns*
  - *indefinite pronouns only.*

Do you remember the difference between an adjective and a pronoun? See Appendix 3.

■ **Indefinite adjectives**

OGNI *(every, each)*
is invariable and is always used with a singular noun; it is a synonym of *tutti/e (all)*. It is placed before the noun.
– Domani **ogni** studente *(tutti gli studenti)* deve portare
  20 euro per la gita a Firenze.
  (Every student must bring 20 euro for the trip to Florence tomorrow.)

QUALCHE *(some, a few)*
is invariable and is always used with a singular noun; it is a synonym of *alcuni (some)*. It is placed before the noun.
  – Rimarremo a Napoli **qualche** giorno *(alcuni giorni)*.
  (We'll stay in Naples for a few days.)

QUALSIASI/QUALCHE *(any, whatever, whichever, a few)*
are synonyms. They mean *tutto/i, non importa chi/quale (every, all, it doesn't matter who/which)*.
They are invariable. They are placed before the noun.
  – **Qualunque/qualsiasi** città tu visiti in Italia, trovi sempre
    qualche opera d'arte interessante.
    (Whichever town you visit in Italy, you always find some interesting work of art.)
▶ In **qualsìasi** the stress goes on the first **i**, not on the **a**.

▪ There are:
– *indefinite adjectives only*
– *indefinite adjectives and pronouns*
– *indefinite pronouns only.*

▪ **Indefinite adjectives** and **pronouns**

ALCUNI/E *(some)*

is variable. When it means *qualche* it is used in the plural form.
It goes before the noun when it is an adjective:

– Ieri sera ho rivisto **alcuni** miei compagni ──▶ *adjective*
(qualche mio compagno) del liceo.
(Yesterday I saw some of my friends
from Grammar School again.)
– **Alcuni** sono invecchiati moltissimo ──▶ *pronoun*
(Some have really aged a lot.)

CIASCUNO *(each, every, any)*

is only used in the singular form and only changes according
to gender. When it is an adjective it means *ogni* and goes
before the noun:

– **Ciascun** lavoratore *(ogni lavoratore)* ──▶ *adjective*
ha diritto a 5 settimane di ferie all'anno.
(Every worker has a right to five weeks' holiday a year.)

▶ When it is an adjective it follows the same rule as the
indefinite article *un/uno/una*:

– ciasc**un l**avorato**re**
(every worker)
– ciasc**una m**aest**ra**
(every primary school teacher)

– ciasc**uno st**udente
(every student)
– ciasc**un'**infermie**ra**
(every nurse)

55

When it is a pronoun it means *ognuno, ogni persona o cosa* (everyone, everthing, each person/thing):

– **Ciascuno** *(ogni persona)* pensi anche agli altri
se vuole migliorare la società. ⟶ *pronoun*
(We should all think of other people if we want to improve society.)

NESSUNO *(no, nobody, anyone)*

is only used in the singular form and only changes according to gender:

– **Nessun** essere umano ha mai messo ⟶ *adjective*
piede su Marte.
(No human being has ever set foot on Mars.)

When it follows the verb it needs the negative adverb *non* (not):

– Non c'è stato **nessun** problema allo ⟶ *adjective*
stadio questa domenica.
(There were no problems at the stadium this Sunday.)

– Ieri sono stato in casa tutto il giorno ⟶ *pronoun*
e non ho visto **nessuno**.
(I stayed at home all day yesterday and I didn't see anyone.)

▷ When it is an adjective it follows the same rule as the indefinite article *un/uno/una*.
See above: ciascuno.

■ There are:
  - *indefinite adjectives only*
  - *indefinite adjectives and pronouns*
  - *indefinite pronouns only.*

■ **Indefinite pronouns**

CHIUNQUE   *(anyone)*

is invariable and is only used in the singular form. It means *qualunque persona*:

- **Chiunque** *(qualunque persona)* può collegare il proprio Pc a Internet.
  (Anyone can connect their Pc to Internet.)

NIENTE/NULLA *(nothing, anything)*

are synonyms. They mean nessuna cosa. They are invariable:

- **Niente/nulla** *(nessuna cosa)* può far paura a quella donna.
  (Nothing can scare that woman.)

When they follow the verb they need the negative adverb *non*:

- Hanno rubato in casa dei vicini, ma **non** mi sono reso conto di **niente/nulla**.
  (They broke into our neighbour's house, but I didn't notice anything.)

OGNUNO   *(everyone)*

is only used in the singular form and changes according to gender. It means *ogni persona*. It is a synonym of ciascuno:

- **Ognuno** *(ogni persona)* deve sapere cosa fare in caso d'incendio.
  (Everyone should know what to do in case of fire.)

56

QUALCOSA *(something)*

is invariable and is always used in the singular form. It means qualche cosa:

- C'è **qualcosa** *(qualche cosa)* nell'aria che mi dà fastidio.
  (There is something in the air that's irritating me.)

QUALCUNO *(someone, anyone, some)*

is only used in the singular form and changes according to gender. It can also mean *qualche persona* or *qualche cosa*:

- **Qualcuno** di voi ha perso questi occhiali?
  (Has anyone [of you] lost these glasses?)
- Ho letto varie novelle di Hesse. **Qualcuna** mi piace, altre no.
  (I've read several short stories by Hesse. Some of them I like, others I don't.)

UNO

is only used in the singular form. It means *una persona* *(a person)*:

- Cosa pensi di **uno** *(una persona)* che dice: "È giusto non pagare più tasse allo stato."?
  (What do you think of someone who says: "We shouldn't pay the State any more taxes"?)

quantifiers (1)
(un po', poco, abbastanza, ecc.) (a little, few, enough, etc.)

57

■ In this unit and in the following we go from *niente (nothing)* to *tutto (everything)*, i.e. the structures are presented in order of increasing quantity.

NIENTE/NULLA see Unità 56.

NESSUNO vedi Unità 55.

POCO *(few, not many/much, little)*

is variable, it is used both as an adjective and as a pronoun. When it is used as an adjective it goes before the noun:

– Ci sono **poche** uova in casa. ⟶ *adjective*
 (*There aren't many eggs in the house.*)

– Silvia ha molti amici ⟶ *pronoun*
 inglesi, io ne ho **pochi**.
 (*Silvia has a lot of English friends, I don't have* many.)

It is also used as an adverb.
 – Ieri mi sono allenato **poco**.
 (*I didn't do much training yesterday.*)

ALCUNI/E vedi Unità 55.

QUALCHE vedi Unità 54.

UN PÒ *(some, a little, a few)*

is a synonym of *qualche* and *alcuni*. When it is placed before the noun it is followed by the preposition **di**:

– Ho **un po' di** soldi in banca, ma sono pochi per comprare una casa.
(I have some money in the bank, but it is not enough to buy a house.)

It is also used as an adverb:

– Ho mangiato **un po'**, ma non abbastanza; ho ancora fame.
(I have eaten a little, but not enough; I'm still hungry.)

VARI/DIVERSI *(several, some)*

used in the plural form and placed before the noun mean *alcuni*. They change according to gender.
They can be both adjectives and pronouns:

– Ho visto **vari** film interessanti ⟶ *adjective*
questa settimana.
(I've seen several interesting films this week.)

– Ci sono studentesse brave qui, però
diverse non studiano abbastanza ⟶ *pronoun*
(There are good female students here, but some of them don't study enough.)

ABBASTANZA *(enough)*

is invariable. It is used both as an adjectives and as a pronoun. It means *a sufficienza*.

– Ho visitato **abbastanza** paesi di lingua ⟶ *adjective*
inglese per poter riconoscere i diversi accenti.
(I have visited enough English speaking countries to be able to recognize the different accent.)

– Ho letto vari libri, ma non **abbastanza** ⟶ *pronoun*
per fare l'esame.
(I've read several books, but not enough to take the esam.)

It is also used as an adverb:
– Ieri mattina ero stanco, ma stanotte ho dormito
abbastanza. *(I was tired yesterday morning, but I got enough sleep last night.)*

Abbastanza has a second meaning as a synonym of *piuttosto* *(rather, quite):*
– Questa mattina ti vedo **abbastanza/piuttosto** allegro.
Cosa hai fatto ieri sera?
(I see you are quite cheerful this morning. What did you do last night?)

PARECCHIO *(quite a few, quite a lot)*

is variable. It indicates a quantity which is bigger than *abbastanza*, but smaller than *molto*. It is an adjective and a pronouns:

– Ho **parecchie** possibilità di essere assunto ⟶ *adjective*
da una agenzia pubblicitaria.
(I have quite a few chances of being employed by an

advertising agency.)

– Sono molti i turisti tedeschi contenti dell'Italia, ma
parecchi non vogliono tornarci. ⟶ *pronoun*
(Many German tourists enjoy Italy,
but quite a few don't want to
come back.)

quantifiers (2)
(molto, tutto, ecc.) (many, all, etc.)

58

MOLTO *(much, many, a lot of)*

is variable, it is used as an adjective and as a pronoun.
It expresses a large quantity but not the whole:

– **Molti** vecchi hanno oggi bisogno di assistenza, ma non
vogliono lasciare la propria casa. ⟶ *adjective*
*(Nowadays many elderly people need assistance
but they do not want to leave their homes.)*

– Ho visitato parecchi posti, ma ce ne sono ancora
molti che vorrei conoscere. ⟶ *pronoun*
*(I have visited quite a few places, but there are still many
I would like to see.)*

It is also used as an adverb:

– Ho camminato **molto** e mi sento stanchissimo.
(I have walked a lot and I feel really tired.)

TANTO *(many, a lot)*

is variable. It is a synonym of *molto* and is used in the same way:

– **Tanti** vecchi hanno oggi bisogno di assistenza, ⟶ *adjective*
ma non vogliono lasciare la propria casa.

– Ho visitato parecchi posti, ma ce ne sono
ancora **tanti** che vorrei conoscere. ⟶ *pronoun*

– Ho camminato **tanto** e mi sento stanchissimo. ⟶ *adverb*

TROPPO *(too much, too many)*

is variable. It indicates excessive quantity. It is used both as an
adjective and as a pronoun.

– Mio figlio di solito non ha molti
compiti da fare, ma per domani
ne ha **troppi**. ⟶ *pronoun*
*(My son doesn't usually have
a lot of homework to do, but
he has far too much for tomorrow.)*

– È **troppo** tempo che non vedo Sandro. ⟶ *adjective*
Stasera gli telefono.
*(I haven't seen Sandro for such a long time. I'm going
to call him this evening.)*

It is also used as an adverb:

– Ho fumato **troppo** questa settimana. Devo cercare di smettere.
(I have smoked too much this week. I must try to give up.)

TUTTO   *(all)*

is variable. It indicates the whole. It is used as an adjective and
as a pronoun:

– Non **tutto** è perduto. *(Not all is lost.)* ⟶ *pronoun*
– **Tutti** sono d'accordo con lui, ma nessuno ⟶ *pronoun*
lo ammette.

(Everyone agrees with him, but no one will admit it.)

When it is used as an adjective it is followed by the definite article.

– **Tutta la** città ha festeggiato la vittoria ⟶ *adjective*
della sua squadra.

(The whole town celebrated its team's victory.)

– **Tutti i** prodotti di quel supermercato ⟶ *adjective*
sono scontati.

(There are discounts on all the products in that supermarket.)

► When **tutto** is followed by a number, there is an $\overset{2}{e}$ after

$\overset{1}{\text{tutti/e}}$, followed by the $\overset{3}{\text{number}}$, the $\overset{4}{\text{article}}$ and then finally

the $\overset{5}{\text{noun}}$:

$\overset{1}{-\text{Tutti}}$ $\overset{2}{e}$ $\overset{3}{5}$ $\overset{4}{i}$ $\overset{5}{\text{figli}}$ di Marta vanno all'università ⟶ *adjective*
(Marta's five children all go to University)

■ Study the picture.

> *Tu sei più alto di me.*

■ The **comparativo di maggioranza**
(more/-er ... than) (see Appendix 3)
of adjectives is formed with the
word **più** (more) followed by the *adjective*.
The second term of comparison is introduced by **di** or **che** (than):
– La Germania è **più** popolata **dell'**Italia.
(Germany has a bigger population than Italy.)

> **DI** is used when the world that follows is

● a **noun**
– Carla è **più** bella **di** sua sorella.
(Carla is prettier than her sister.)

● a **personal pronoun**
– Giorgio è **più** vecchio di **me**. (Giorgio is older than me.)

> **CHE** is used when the word that follows is

● an **adjective**
– Lino è **più** simpatico **che attraente**.
(Lino is nice rather than attractive.)

● a **verb in the infinitive**
– Stare in vacanza è **più** bello che lavorare.
(Being on holiday is better than working.)

● a **prepositional phrase**
– Pavarotti è **più** bravo dal vivo **che su disco**.
(Pavarotti is better live than recorded.)

● an **adverb**
– Certi studenti rispondono alle domande **più** meccanicamente
che intelligentemente.
(Some students answer questions more mechanically than
intelligently.)

Che is also used when the comparison is between

- **two nouns** which are *not subjects*:
  - In televisione vedo **più film che programmi** di informazione.
    (I watch more films than documentaries on television)

▶ For the use of the subjunctive with the comparativo di maggioranza + a relative clause introduced by **di quanto** (than) see Unità 70:
  - Flavio è **più** vecchio **di quanto** credessi.
    (Flavio is older than I thought.)

■ The **comparativo di minoranza** *(less... than, not as... as)* (see Appendix 3) is formed in the same way as the *comparativo di maggioranza*, using the word **meno** *(less)* instead of *più*:
  - Il tedesco è **meno** difficile del russo.
    (German is less difficult than Russian.)

■ The **comparativo di uguaglianza** *(as... as)* (see Appendix 3) is formed by using:

● **(tanto)** + adjective, **quanto** + adjective, when comparing two *adjectives*:
  - Il mio barbiere è **(tanto)** bravo **quanto** simpatico.
    (My barber is not only friendly but also very good.)

● **(tanto)... quanto** or **(così)... come** when comparing *nouns, pronouns* and *verbs* in the infinitive:
  - Il lago è **(tanto)** riposante **quanto** la montagna.
    (It is just relaxing to go to a lake as going to the mountains.)
  - Rossana è **(tanto)** alta **quanto** me.
    (Rossana is just as tall as me.)
  - Leggere è **(così)** stimolante **come** andare al cinema.
    (Reading is just as stimulating as going to the cinema.)

▶ **Tanto** and **così** can often be left out.

superlative adjectives (relativo and assoluto) **60**
(il più bello, il più alto, grandissimo)
(the most beautiful, the tallest, very big)

■ Study the picture.

Nicola è *il più alto* di tutti.

Is anyone taller than Nicola in his
class? And in the world?

■ The **superlativo relativo** *(the most/-est, least)* is formed with
the *definite article* and the *comparativo (di maggioranza or
minoranza)*.
It indicates the characteristic of a person or object by
comparing it with other people or objects:
– Davide è **il** musicista **più esperto** dell'orchestra.
  (Davide is the most experienced musician in the orchestra.)
– È **lo** studente **meno preparato** della scuola.
  (He is the student who studies the least in the whole school.)

▶ The noun can sometimes follow the adjective, however the
article is always placed before the adjective:
– Roma è **la più grande** città d'Italia.
  (Rome is the largest city in Italy.)

● The second element can be introduced by **di** but also by **fra**
or by **che + subjunctive**:
– È l'appartamento più ampio **dell'**edificio.
  (It is the largest flat in the building.)
– Lo Zio Camillo è il più ricco **fra** tutti i miei parenti.
  (Uncle Camillo is the richest of all my relatives.)
– È la macchina più veloce **che** io **abbia** (mai) **avuto**.
  (It's the fastest car I've (ever) had.)

▶ **Fra** cannot be used when the word that follows is a *noun
of place*.
– Londra è la più popolata città **d'**Europa.
  (London is the most populated city in Europe.)

60

▶ For the use of the subjunctive with the superlativo relativo see Unità 70.

■ Study the picture.

Sei **bellissima***!*

Is anyone prettier than this girl?
We do not know, as there are no comparisons in the sentence.

■ The **superlativo assoluto** (*very/really* + *adjective*) is formed by adding the suffix **-issimo** to the adjective.
It emphasizes the characteristic of a person or an object without making any comparison:
– Il film di ieri sera era noios**issimo**.
   (The film yesterday evening was very boring.)
– La storia è una materia interessant**issima**.
   (History is a really interesting subject.)

The sentences above could also be said in the following way:
– Il film di ieri sera era **molto** noioso.
– La storia è una materia **molto** interessante.

The structure with **-issimo** however is very common and is particularly expressive.

▶ Adjectives ending in -co and **-go** add an **h**.
   lungo ⟶ lung**h**issimo *(very long)*
   bianco ⟶ bianc**h**issimo *(really white)*.

irregular comparatives and superlatives - other forms **61**

(buono, migliore, ottimo, ecc.) (good, better, best, etc.)

■ Irregular comparatives and superlatives

forma di base	comparativo	superl. relativo	superl. assoluto
buono (good)	**migliore** (better)	**il migliore** (the best)	**ottimo** (excellent)
cattivo (bad)	**peggiore** (worse)	**il peggiore** (the worst)	**pessimo** (the absolute worst)
grande (big, old, great)	**maggiore** (bigger, elder, greater)	**il maggiore** (the biggest, the eldest, the greater)	**massimo** (maximum)
piccolo (small, young)	**minore** (smaller, younger)	**il minore** (the smallest, the youngest)	**minimo** (minimum)

– È la pizza **peggiore** che abbia mai assaggiato.
 (It's the worst pizza I've ever eaten.)

▶ In addition to the irregular forms there are also regular forms which are generally used to indicate human qualities.
 – Mia mamma dice che sono **più cattivo** di mio fratello.
  (My mum says I'm naughtier than my brother.)

● When talking about sizes the adjectives **grande** and **piccolo** are used:
 – La Fiat Punto è **più piccola** della Volvo 850.
  (A Fiat Punto is smaller than a Volvo 850.)

When talking about age it is better to use **maggiore** and **minore**.
 – Mio fratello **maggiore** lavora in una ditta edile.
  (My elder brother works for a construction firm.)

61

■ In modern Italian the *superlativo assoluto* can also be expressed with prefixes, i.e. **arci-, iper, stra-, super-, ultra-**.
  – È un apparecchio **ultraveloce**. *(It's an ultra fast plane.)*
  – Quell'uomo è **straricco**. *(That man is really loaded.)*
  – È un'opera **arcinota**. *(It's a very famous opera.)*
  – Luigi è un lavoratore **superefficiente**.
    (Luigi is a super-efficient worker.)
  – Come mi stressi! Sei così **iperattivo**!
    (You really stress me out! You're so hyperactive!)

▶ The *superlativo assoluto* can sometimes be expressed by repeating the adjective which indicates the quality:
  – Vivo in un appartamento **piccolo piccolo**.
    (I live in a really tiny flat.)

■ Different expressions can be used to emphasise the comparative, i.e.:
  molto, assai, notevolmente, estremamente, etc.
  (much, far, a lot, etc.)

▶ These words go before **più**.
  – Il tuo nuovo ragazzo è **molto più** interessante di Mauro.
    (Your new boyfriend is far more interesting than Mauro)

  – La soluzione di questo problema risulta **estremamente più** complessa di quanto pensassi.
    (The solution to this problem appears to be much more complicated than I thought.)

▪ Adverbs of manner

forma di base	compar. di maggior. e minoranza	superl. relativo	superl. assoluto
giustamente (rightly)	**più/meno giustamente** (more/less rightly)	**nel modo più giusto nella maniera più giusta** (in the best way)	**giustissimamente molto giustamente**

– Ti farò arrivare il pacco **nel modo più veloce**.
  (I'll send you the parcel the fastest way possible)
– Ricordati di parlagli **più chiaramente** di quanto tu abbia fatto finora. (Remember to speak to him more clearly than you have done so far.)

▪ Irregular forms

forma di base	compar. di maggior. e minoranza	superlativo	superlativo assoluto
bene (good)	**meglio** (better)	**nel modo migliore nella maniera migliore** (in the best way)	**benissimo** (very well)
male (badly)	**peggio** (worse)	**nel modo peggiore nella maniera peggiore** (in the worst way)	**malissimo** (very badly)
molto (a lot)	**più** (more)	**il più possibile** (as much as possible)	**moltissimo** (very much)
poco (litttle)	**meno** (less, fewer)	**il meno possibile** (the least possible, the fewest, as little as)	**pochissimo** (very little/ few)

– Mangia **il più possibile**! Sei così magra!
  (Eat as much as you can! You're so thin!)
– L'esame mi è andato **malissimo**. (My esam went really badly.)

62

■ **Other adverbs**

forma di base	compar. di maggior. e minoranza	superlativo relativo	superlativo assoluto
presto *(soon, early)*	**più/meno presto** *(sooner, earlier, less soon/earlier)*	**il più presto possibile** *(as soon as possible)*	**prestissimo** *(very soon/earlier)*
spesso *(often)*	**più/meno spesso** *(more/less often)*	**il più spesso possibile** *(as often as possible)*	**spessissimo** *(very often)*

– Cerca di telefonare a tua madre **più spesso**.
  (Try and phone your mother more often.)
– Questa mattina mi sono alzato **prestissimo**.
  (I got up really early this morning.)

■ The **comparative** of adverbs can be modified by using **molto** or **assai**.

– In treno arrivo a casa **molto/assai più rapidamente** che in macchina.
  (I get home much faster by train than by car.)

■ Apart from the structure **nel modo più** giusto, etc., the superlativo relativo can also be expressed with: **nel più** giusto **dei modi** *(in the best of ways)*, etc.

– Durante un colloquio di lavoro bisogna cercare di esprimersi **nel più corretto dei modi**.
  (During an interview one must try to express oneself as correctly as possible.)

imperative - form   63

(mangia!, andate!, non andare!) (eat!, go!, don't go!)

■ Study the picture.

Raccogli i tuoi giocattoli!

■ **Affirmative form** of the **imperative** for second person singular and first and second person plural.

● **Regular verbs**

I - ARE: cantare (sing)	II - ERE: prendere (take)	III a- IRE: sentire (hear)	III b- IRE: finire (finish)
cant **-a!**	prend **-i!**	sent **-i!**	fin **-isci!**
cant **-iamo!**	prend **-iamo!**	sent **-iamo!**	fin **-iamo!**
cant **-ate!**	prend **-ete!**	sent **-ite!**	fin **-ite!**

● **Verbs *essere* and *avere***

avere	essere
abbi!	sii!
abbiamo!	siamo!
abbiate!	siate!

– **Sii** più determinato e vedrai che otterrai maggiori successi!
  (Be more determined and you'll see that you'll be more successful!)

63

● **Irregular verbs**

andare	va'! andiamo! andate!	dire	di'! diciamo! dite!	sapere	sappi! sappiamo! sappiate!
dare	da'! diamo! date!	fare	fa'! facciamo! fate!	stare	sta'! stiamo! state!

– **Andate** a casa subito, sta per piovere!
  (Go home straight away, it's going to rain!)

■ For the polite **affirmative form** of the **imperative** (lei - Loro) the *present subjunctive* is used.

● **Regular verbs**

I - ARE: cantare (sing)	II - ERE: prendere (take)	III - IRE: sentire (hear)	III - IRE: finire (finish)
(Lei) cant **-i!** (Loro) cant **-ino!**	prend **-a!** prend **-ano!**	sent **-a!** sent **-ano!**	fin **-isca!** fin **-iscano!**

– **Prenda** un caffè, Signora! Glielo offro con piacere.
  (Please have a coffee! It's on me.)

▶ The polite form with **Loro** is very rarely used in modern Italian. See Unità 38.

▶ For irregular verbs see Unità 66.

■ For the **negative structure** of the **imperative non** is placed before the forms used in the affirmative.

▶ For the second person singular **non + infinito** is used.

I - ARE: cantare	II - ERE: prendere	III a - IRE: sentire	III b - IRE: finire
non cant **-are!** non cant **-i!** non cant **-iamo!** non cant **-ate!** non cant **-ino!**	non prend **-ere!** non prend **-a!** non prend **-iamo!** non prend **-ete!** non prend **-ano!**	non sent **-ire!** non sent **-a!** non sent **-iamo!** non sent **-ite!** non sent **-ano!**	non fin **-ire!** non fin **-isca!** non fin **-iamo!** non fin **-ite!** non fin **-iscano!**

– **Non aprire** la finestra, fa troppo freddo!
  (Don't open the window, it's too cold!)
– Per favore, **non urlate**, voglio riposare!
  (Please don't shout, I want to have a rest!)

imperative with pronouns
(mangialo!, andateci!, non parlargli!)
(eat it!, go there!, don't speak to him!)

64

■ Study the picture.

Fermatevi!

■ **Unstressed object pronouns**, **ne** and **ci** follow the second person singular and the first and second person plural:
  – Ricordiamo**ci** di chiudere la finestra quando usciamo!
    (We must remember to close the window when we go out!)
  – Passa**mi** l'acqua per favore! *(Pass me the water, please!)*
  – Togliete**vi** le scarpe prima di entrare in casa!
    (Take your shoes off before you come into the house!)
  – Se vedi Giovanna, non parlar**le** della festa per il suo compleanno!
    (If you see Giovanna, don't tell her about her birthday party!)

■ **Unstressed object pronouns**, **ne** and **ci** are placed before the polite forms Lei and Loro:
  – **Lo** guardi bene e **mi** dica se lo riconosce!
    (Take a good look and tell me if you recognize him!)

■ Some irregular verbs in the second person singular, when followed by **unstressed object pronouns**, **ne** or **ci** double the consonant of the pronoun, e.g.:

andare ⟶ Va**cci** piano con quel vino! *(Go steady on that wine!)*

dare ⟶ Da**lle** una mano, non riesce a sollevare la valigia!
    (Give her a hand, she can't lift her suitcase!)

dire ⟶ Di**mmi** come ti chiami! *(Tell me your name!)*

fare ⟶ Fa**mmi** un favore, spegni la luce!
    (Do me a favour, switch off the light!)

stare ⟶ Sta**cci** attento, è uno sport pericoloso!
    (Be careful, it's a dangerous sport!)

▶ Exception: there is no double **g** with **gli**:
  – Da**gli** il mio numero di telefono e di**gli** di chiamarmi presto!
    (Give him my phone number and tell him to call me soon!)

■ The **imperative** only has one tense, the present.

■ It is used to express

● **orders**

> *Torna* subito qui!

(Come back here right away!)

● **prohibitions**

(Do not speak to the driver.)

● **invitations**

> *Smetti* di fumare, credimi è meglio per tutti!

(Give up smoking, believe me, it's better for us all!)

● **suggestions**

> Su, *facciamo* qualcosa, *andiamo* al cinema!

(Come on, let's do something, let's go to the cinema!)

● **request/appeals**

> Ti prego: *non lasciarmi!*

(Please don't leave me!)

(che io mangi, che tu vada)

■ **Regular verbs**

I - ARE: cantare *(sing)*		II - ERE: vedere *(see)*	
che (io)	cant **-i**	che (io)	ved **-a**
che (tu)	cant **-i**	che (tu)	ved **-a**
che (lui, lei, Lei)	cant **-i**	che (lui, lei, Lei)	ved **-a**
che (noi)	cant **-iamo**	che (noi)	ved **-iamo**
che (voi)	cant **-iate**	che (voi)	ved **-iate**
che (loro)	cant **-ino**	che (loro)	ved **-ano**

III a - IRE: sentire *(hear)*		III b - IRE: finire *(finish)*	
che (io)	sent **-a**	che (io)	fin **-isc -a**
che (tu)	sent **-a**	che (tu)	fin **-isc -a**
che (lui, lei, Lei)	sent **-a**	che (lui, lei, Lei)	fin **-isc -a**
che (noi)	sent **-iamo**	che (noi)	fin **-iamo**
che (voi)	sent **-iate**	che (voi)	fin **-iate**
che (loro)	sent **-ano**	che (loro)	fin **-isc -ano**

– Desidero che mia sorella **finisca** bene gli esami.
 (I hope my sister does well in her last exams.)
– Non credo che il cantante del gruppo musicale di
 Gianluca **canti** nel modo migliore.
 *(I don't think the vocalist in Gianluca's band sings
 particularly well.)*

■ For the verbs *essere* and *avere*: see Unità 68.

■ **Irregular verbs**

potere *(can)*		volere *(want)*	
che (io)	**possa**	che (io)	**voglia**
che (tu)	**possa**	che (tu)	**voglia**
che (lui, lei, Lei)	**possa**	che (lui, lei, Lei)	**voglia**
che (noi)	**possiamo**	che (noi)	**vogliamo**
che (voi)	**possiate**	che (voi)	**vogliate**
che (loro)	**possano**	che (loro)	**vogliano**

dovere *(must)*		sapere *(know)*	
che (io)	**debba**	che (io)	**sappia**
che (tu)	**debba**	che (tu)	**sappia**
che (lui, lei, Lei)	**debba**	che (lui, lei, Lei)	**sappia**
che (noi)	**dobbiamo**	che (noi)	**sappiamo**
che (voi)	**dobbiate**	che (voi)	**sappiate**
che (loro)	**debbano**	che (loro)	**sappiano**

piacere *(like)*		bere *(drink)*	
che (io)	**piaccia**	che (io)	**beva**
che (tu)	**piaccia**	che (tu)	**beva**
che (lui, lei, Lei)	**piaccia**	che (lui, lei, Lei)	**beva**
che (noi)	**piacciano**	che (noi)	**beviamo**
che (voi)	**piacciate**	che (voi)	**beviate**
che (loro)	**piacciano**	che (loro)	**bevano**

andare *(go)*		stare *(be, stay)*	
che (io)	**vada**	che (io)	**stia**
che (tu)	**vada**	che (tu)	**stia**
che (lui, lei, Lei)	**vada**	che (lui, lei, Lei)	**stia**
che (noi)	**andiamo**	che (noi)	**stiamo**
che (voi)	**andiate**	che (voi)	**stiate**
che (loro)	**vadano**	che (loro)	**stiano**

fare *(do, make)*		dare *(give)*	
che (io)	**faccia**	che (io)	**dia**
che (tu)	**faccia**	che (tu)	**dia**
che (lui, lei, Lei)	**faccia**	che (lui, lei, Lei)	**dia**
che (noi)	**facciamo**	che (noi)	**diamo**
che (voi)	**facciate**	che (voi)	**diate**
che (loro)	**facciano**	che (loro)	**diano**

dire (say)		**uscire** (go out)	
che (io)	**dica**	che (io)	**esca**
che (tu)	**dica**	che (tu)	**esca**
che (lui, lei, Lei)	**dica**	che (lui, lei, Lei)	**esca**
che (noi)	**diciamo**	che (noi)	**usciamo**
che (voi)	**diciate**	che (voi)	**usciate**
che (loro)	**dicano**	che (loro)	**escano**

tenere (keep, hold)		**porre** (put, place)	
che (io)	**tenga**	che (io)	**ponga**
che (tu)	**tenga**	che (tu)	**ponga**
che (lui, lei, Lei)	**tenga**	che (lui, lei, Lei)	**ponga**
che (noi)	**teniamo**	che (noi)	**poniamo**
che (voi)	**teniate**	che (voi)	**poniate**
che (loro)	**tengano**	che (loro)	**pongano**

trarre (pull, draw)		**venire** (come)	
che (io)	**tragga**	che (io)	**venga**
che (tu)	**tragga**	che (tu)	**venga**
che (lui, lei, Lei)	**tragga**	che (lui, lei, Lei)	**venga**
che (noi)	**traiamo**	che (noi)	**veniamo**
che (voi)	**traiate**	che (voi)	**veniate**
che (loro)	**traggano**	che (loro)	**vengano**

– Spero che **possiate** venire presto a trovarci.
  (I hope you'll able to visit us soon.)
– Tua madre vuole che i tuoi cugini **escano** con noi domani
  sera.
  *(Your mother wants your cousins to come out with us
  tomorrow evening.)*

▶ The **present subjunctive** is based on the form of the present
  indicative.

■ **Regular verbs**

I - ARE: cantare *(sing)*		II - ERE: vedere *(see)*	
che (io)	cant **-assi**	che (io)	ved **-essi**
che (tu)	cant **-assi**	che (tu)	ved **-essi**
che (lui, lei, Lei)	cant **-asse**	che (lui, lei, Lei)	ved **-esse**
che (noi)	cant **-assimo**	che (noi)	ved **-essimo**
che (voi)	cant **-aste**	che (voi)	ved **-este**
che (loro)	cant **-assero**	che (loro)	ved **-essero**

III a - IRE: sentire *(hear)*		III b - IRE: finire *(finish)*	
che (io)	sent **-issi**	che (io)	fin **-issi**
che (tu)	sent **-issi**	che (tu)	fin **-issi**
che (lui, lei, Lei)	sent **-isse**	che (lui, lei, Lei)	fin **-isse**
che (noi)	sent **-issimo**	che (noi)	fin **-issimo**
che (voi)	sent **-iste**	che (voi)	fin **-iste**
che (loro)	sent **-issero**	che (loro)	fin **-issero**

– Pensavo che i tuoi amici **giocassero** in una squadra di pallavolo.
(I thought your friends played in a volleyball team.)
– Alcuni anni fa volevo che i miei genitori **andassero** in vacanza sulle Dolomiti.
(A few years ago I wanted my parents to go to the Dolomites for their holidays.)

■ For the verbs **essere** and **avere**: see Unità 68.

■ Some verbs which are irregular in the *imperfect indicative* maintain the same elements in the *imperfect subjunctive*.

dire *(say)*		fare *(do, make)*	
che (io)	**dicessi**	che (io)	**facessi**
che (tu)	**dicessi**	che (tu)	**facessi**
che (lui, lei, Lei)	**dicesse**	che (lui, lei, Lei)	**facesse**
che (noi)	**dicessimo**	che (noi)	**facessimo**
che (voi)	**diceste**	che (voi)	**faceste**
che (loro)	**dicessero**	che (loro)	**facessero**

porre *(put, place)*		**tradurre** *(translate)*	
che (io)	**ponessi**	che (io)	**traducessi**
che (tu)	**ponessi**	che (tu)	**traducessi**
che (lui, lei, Lei)	**ponesse**	che (lui, lei, Lei)	**traducesse**
che (noi)	**ponessimo**	che (noi)	**traducessimo**
che (voi)	**poneste**	che (voi)	**traduceste**
che (loro)	**ponessero**	che (loro)	**traducessero**

trarre *(pull, draw)*	
che (io)	**traessi**
che (tu)	**traessi**
che (lui, lei, Lei)	**traesse**
che (noi)	**traessimo**
che (voi)	**traeste**
che (loro)	**traessero**

▶ Also: che io **bevessi**.

■ **Dare** and **stare**

dare *(give)*		**stare** *(be, stay)*	
che (io)	**dessi**	che (io)	**stessi**
che (tu)	**dessi**	che (tu)	**stessi**
che (lui, lei, Lei)	**desse**	che (lui, lei, Lei)	**stesse**
che (noi)	**dessimo**	che (noi)	**stessimo**
che (voi)	**deste**	che (voi)	**steste**
che (loro)	**dessero**	che (loro)	**stessero**

▶ The forms for the *first* and *second person singular* are the same in the *imperfect subjunctive*.
It is therefore necessary to express the subject of the sentence:
– Michela non capiva come **io potessi** lavorare tanto.
  (Michela couldn't understand how I could work so hard.)

■ Study these examples.
  – Spero che tu **sia stata** bene in vacanza e che non **abbia avuto** problemi.
    (I hope you had a good time on holiday and didn't have any problems.)
  – Gli esperti pensano che l'inflazione non **sia cresciuta** molto il mese scorso.
    (Experts believe inflation did not rise much last month.)

■ The **past subjunctive** is formed with the *present subjunctive* of *essere* and *avere* plus the *past participle* of the verb.

■ **Present subjunctive** of the verbs *essere* and *avere*

avere		essere	
che (io)	**abbia**	che (io)	**sia**
che (tu)	**abbia**	che (tu)	**sia**
che (lui, lei, Lei)	**abbia**	che (lui, lei, Lei)	**sia**
che (noi)	**abbiamo**	che (noi)	**siamo**
che (voi)	**abbiate**	che (voi)	**siate**
che (loro)	**abbiano**	che (loro)	**siano**

■ Study these examples.
  – Credevo che **fossi** già **arrivata** a casa, per questo ti ho chiamato.
    (I thought you were already home, that's why I called you.)
  – Mi sarebbe piaciuto che Rossana **avesse preso** il lavoro che gli avevano offerto.*(I would have liked Rossana to take the job they offered her.)*

■ The **past perfect subjunctive** is formed with the *imperfect subjunctive* of *essere* and *avere* plus the *past participle* of the verb.

■ **Imperfect subjunctive** of the verbs *essere* and *avere*

avere		essere	
che (io)	**avessi**	che (io)	**fossi**
che (tu)	**avessi**	che (tu)	**fossi**
che (lui, lei, Lei)	**avesse**	che (lui, lei, Lei)	**fosse**
che (noi)	**avessimo**	che (noi)	**fossimo**
che (voi)	**aveste**	che (voi)	**foste**
che (loro)	**avessero**	che (loro)	**fosssero**

subjunctive - use (1)
(penso che l'inglese sia facile, ecc.)
(I think English is easy, etc.)

69

■ The **subjunctive** is used after

● verbs and phrases which express **feelings**:
temere, avere paura, piacere/dispiacere, sperare, essere contento/felice, vergognarsi, ecc. (fear, be afraid, be pleased/sorry, hope, be glad/happy, be ashamed, etc.)
   – **Temo** che Mauro **arrivi** in ritardo.
     (I'm afraid Mauro will be late.)
   – **Sono contento** che il tuo libro **abbia** successo.
     (I'm pleased your book is successful)
   – Mi **dispiace** che tu non **possa** venire in vacanza con noi.
     (I'm sorry you can't come on holiday with us.)

● verbs and phrases which express **opinion**:
credere, pensare, ritenere, supporre, avere l'impressione, ecc. (believe, think, consider, suppose, have the impression, etc.)
   – **Penso** che Marcello Mastroianni **sia** il miglior attore italiano.
     (I think Marcello Mastroianni is the best Italian actor.)
   – **Ho l'impressione** che Matteo non **conosca** molto bene lo spagnolo.
     (I have the feeling that Matteo doesn't know Spanish very well.)

▶ In spoken Italian the indicative is often used instead of the subjunctive, even though it is not correct:
   – **Credo** che **va** bene così. *(I think that's fine like that.)*

● verbs which express **volition**:
volere, desiderare, preferire, ordinare, vietare, permettere, ecc. (want, would like, prefer, expect, order, forbid, allow, etc.)
   – **Desidero** che tu mi **dica** la verità! *(I want you to tell me the truth!)*
   – **Non permetto** che qualcuno **parli** male del mio paese, senza conoscerlo.
     (I won't let anyone speak badly of my country when they know nothing about it.)

- verbs and phrases which express **doubt**:
  dubitare, non essere sicuro/certo, ecc.
  (doubt, unsure/uncertain, etc.)
  - **Non sono sicuro** che la Nazionale italiana di calcio **possa** vincere contro il Brasile.
    (I'm not sure if the Italian football team can beat Brazil.)
- **impersonal verbs**:
  basta, bisogna, conviene, occorre, pare, può darsi, sembra, ecc. (be enough, need, be better, have to, seem, may, look like, etc.)
  - **Sembra** che ci **siano** molti nuovi iscritti ai corsi d'italiano.
    (There seems to be a lot of new enrolments for the Italian courses.)
  - **Bisogna** che l'Italia **risolva** i problemi del Meridione.
    (Italy needs to solve the problems in the South.)
- the verb **essere** in the **impersonal form** (è, era. etc.)
  + adjective, adverb or **noun**:
  - **È meglio** che tu **venga** in Italia, se vuoi imparare l'italiano veramente bene.
    (You had better come to Italy if you want to learn Italian really well.)
  - **È giusto** che ogni bambino **possa** frequentare la scuola gratuitamente.
    (It is right that every child has the chance to attend school free of charge.)
  - **È importante** che un giovane **impari** diverse lingue straniere.
    (It is important for a young person to learn several foreign languages.)
- The verb **sapere** is followed by the subjunctive only when it is used in the negative form:
  - **Non so** se Jean **sia** francese o belga.
    (I don't know whether Jean is French or Belgian.)
- When the verb **dire** is used in the impersonal form **si dice/dicono** it is always followed by the subjunctive.
  - **Si dice/dicono** che in Italia si **viva** meglio che in molti altri paesi.
    (They say/It is said that the way of life in Italy is better than in many other countries.)

subjunctive - use (2)
(affinché, benché, ecc.) (so that, although, etc.)

70

■ The **subjunctive** is used after

AFFINCHÉ *(so that)*

– L'idraulico ha finito la riparazione velocemente, **affinché** gli inquilini **possano** nuovamente aprire l'acqua.
(The plumber finished the repair quickly so that the tenants can turn the water on again.)

BENCHÉ, MALGRADO, NONOSTANTE, SEBBENE, *(although, even though)*, which have basically the same meaning and use:

– **Benché** non **sappia** nuotare, Carlo si è tuffato dove l'acqua è profonda.
(Although unable to swim, Carlo dived in where the water is deep.)

– **Nonostante** non **conosca** una parola di turco, sono andato in vacanza in Turchia.
(Even though I don't know a word in Turkish, I went to Turkey on holiday.)

PURCHÉ, A PATTO CHE, A CONDIZIONE CHE, *(as long as, provided, on condition that)*, which have basically the same meaning and use:

– Vengo a trovarti, **a condizione che** tu non **prepari** niente di speciale. *(I'll come and see you as long as you don't start preparing anything special.)*

– Compreremo una nuova macchina a fine anno, **purché riusciamo** a risparmiare tutti i soldi necessari.
(We'll buy a new car at the end of the year, provided we can save up enough money.)

A MENO CHE NON *(unless)*

– **A meno che non decidiamo** di andare al mare, rimarremo in città.
(Unless we decide to go to the seaside, we'll stay in town.)

SENZA CHE   *(without)*

– Donatella incontra spesso Adriano, senza che suo marito lo **sappia**.
(Donatella often sees Adriano without her husband knowing.)

PRIMA CHE   *(before)*

– **Prima che nasca** il figlio di Patricia, gli prenderò un regalino.
(Before Patricia's baby is born, I'll buy him a little present)

NEL CASO CHE   *(in case)*

– **Nel caso che** nessuno ve lo **abbia detto**, vi avverto che le lezioni ricominceranno il primo novembre.
(In case nobody has told you, I just want to tell you that the lessons will start again on November 1.)

■ The subjunctive is used in a **relative clause**

● when there is a **superlativo relativo** in the main clause:
  – È il libro **più** bello che io **abbia** letto.
  (It's the best book I've ever read.)

● with **di quanto** and a comparative in the main clause:
  – Questo film è **più** interessante **di quanto pensassi**.
  (This film is more interesting than I thought.)

● to express a requirement. In the main clause there often is a verb like cercare, desiderare, aspettare, volere, avere bisogno, ecc. *(look for, would like, expect, want, need, etc.)*:
  – Stefano **ha bisogno** di una compagna **che** gli **dedichi** molto tempo.
  (Stefano needs a partner who will devote a lot of time to him)
  – **Cerco** un computer più veloce del mio, **che mi faccia** risparmiare tempo.
  (I'm looking for a faster computer than mine, that will save me time.)

● with some **indefinite** adjectives and pronouns: *chiunque, comunque, dovunque, qualunque (anyone, anyhow, anywhere, anything)*:
  – **Chiunque** ti **conosca**, sa che sei un bugiardo.
  (Anyone that knows you knows you're a liar.)
  – In Italia **dovunque** uno **vada**, occorrono sempre molti soldi.
  (Wherever you go in Italy, you always need a lot of money.)

sequences of tenses - with the indicative   **71**

(sono sicuro che tu mangi molto, ecc.) (I'm sure you eat a lot, etc.)

■ If the verb in the main clause is in the **present indicative** and

● the subordinate clause expresses a *future time,* i.e. the action in the subordinate clause happens after the action in the main clause, then the **present** or **future indicative** is used:

adesso   **domani**

– **Sono certo** che domani **vado/andrò** al mare.
  (I'm sure I'm going to the seaside tomorrow.)

● the subordinate clause expresses *contemporary time,* i.e. the two actions happen at the same time, then the **present indicative** is used:

ieri   **adesso**   domani

– **So** che Lucia **studia/sta studiando** pianoforte.
  (I know that Lucia is learning to play the piano.)

● the subordinate clause expresses an *earlier time,* i.e. the action in the subordinate clause happened *first,* then the **passato prossimo/remoto** or **imperfect indicative** is used:

ieri   adesso

– **Ti dico** che ieri Gloria si **è laureata**. Non mi credi?
  (I'm telling you that Gloria graduated yesterday. Don't you believe me?)

■ If the verb in the main clause is in the **passato prossimo/remoto**, **imperfect** or **past perfect indicative** and

● the subordinate expresses a *future time,* i.e. the action in the subordinate clause happens *after* the action in the main clause, then the **perfect conditional** is used:

71

Aprile 1989   **Novembre 1989**

* |--| * |

– Nell'aprile del 1989 **ero sicuro** che **avrei iniziato** a lavorare in una scuola di montagna in novembre.
(In April 1989 I knew I would start working in a school in the mountains in November.)

● the subordinate clause expresses *contemporary time*, i.e. the two actions happen *at the same time*, then the **passato prossimo/remoto**, **imperfect** or **past perfect indicative** is used:

anni fa   adesso

* |_|---| * |

– Anni fa mia madre mi **diceva** spesso che mio padre **ballava** molto bene. *(Years ago my mother often used to tell me that my father danced really well.)*

● the subordinate clause expresses an *earlier time*, i.e. the action in the subordinate clause happened *first*, then the **past perfect indicative** is used:

ore 20   ore 24

* |--| * |

– Quando arrivò era quasi mezzanotte e **sapevo** che **aveva** già **cenato**.
(When he arrived it was almost midnight and I knew he had already had dinner.)

sequences of tenses - with the subjunctive (1) | 72

(spero che tu mangi, ecc.) (I hope you'll eat, etc.)

■ If the verb in the main clause is in the **present indicative** and

● the subordinate clause expresses a *future time*, i.e. the action in the subordinate clause happens *after* the action in the main clause, then the **present subjunctive** or **future indicative** is used:

adesso   **domani**

   – **Spero** che domani Suly non **vada/andrà** a lavorare.
   (I hope Suly won't go to work tomorrow.)

● the subordinate clause expresses *contemporary time*, i.e. the two actions happen at the *same time*, then the **present subjunctive** is used:

ieri   **adesso**   domani

   – Non **so** che cosa **faccia/stia facendo** Giovanni in questo momento. *(I don't know what Giovanni is doing at the moment.)*

● the subordinate clause expresses an *earlier time*, i.e. the action in the subordinate clause happens *first*, then **the past** subjunctive is used:

ieri   adesso

   – **Penso** che ieri Fausto **abbia fatto** un giro nei boschi con i suoi figli. *(I think Fausto went to the woods with his children yesterday.)*

■ If the verb in the main clause in the **conditional** and

● the subordinate clause expresses a *future time*, i.e. the action in the subordinate clause happens *after* the action in the main clause, then the **imperfect subjunctive** is used:

149

adesso   **domani**

```
     *                                          *
 ----|--------------------------------------------|
     |                                   |_____|
```

- Mi **piacerebbe** che tu **smettessi** di lavorare presto domani per andare al ristorante insieme.
  (I'd be really pleased if you could finish work early tomorrow so we can go to the restaurant together.)

● the subordinate clause expresses *contemporary time*, i.e. the two actions happen at the *same time*, then the **imperfect subjunctive** is used:

ieri   **adesso**   domani

```
  *                 |                    *
 -|-----------------|--------------------
  |_____|
```

- **Vorrei** che qualcuno mi **aiutasse** a correggere gli esami.
  (I wish someone would help me correct the exams.)

● the subordinate clause expresses an *earlier time*, i.e. the action in the subordinate clause happened *first*, then the **past perfect subjunctive** is used:

l'anno scorso   adesso

```
  *                                         *
 -|-----------------------------------------|
  |_____|
```

- **Vorrei** che l'anno scorso vi **foste iscritti** all'università.
  (I wish you had enrolled at University last year.)

- If the verb in the main clause is in the **passato prossimo/remoto**, **imperfect** o **past perfect indicative** and

- the subordinate clause expresses a *future time*, i.e. the action in the subordinate clause happens *after* the action in the main clause, then the **perfect conditional** is used:

Marzo 1990   **Ottobre 1990**   adesso

– Nel marzo del 1990 **credevo** che Fabrizio **avrebbe iniziato** il servizio militare agli inizi di ottobre.
(In March 1990 I thought Fabrizio would start his military service at the beginning of October.)

- the subordinate clause expresses a *contemporary time*, i.e. the two actions happen *same time*, then the **imperfect subjunctive** is used:

anni fa   adesso

– In Italia fino a pochi anni fa, molti uomini **pretendevano** che le donne **stessero** in casa con i figli e non **lavorassero**.
(Up to a few years ago many men in Italy expected women to stay home with the children and not go out to work.)

- the subordinate clause expresses an *earlier time*, i.e. the action in the subordinate clause happened *first*, then the **past perfect subjunctive** is used:

ore 20   ore 24   adesso

– Quando arrivò era quasi mezzanotte e **pensai** che **avesse** già **cenato**
(When he got home it was almost midnight and I thought he had already had dinner.)

73

■ If the verb in the main clause is in the **perfect conditional** and

● the subordinate clause expresses a *future time*, i.e. the action in the subordinate clause happens *after* the action in the main clause, then the **imperfect subjunctive** or **future indicative** is used:

una settimana fa   **giorno dopo**   adesso

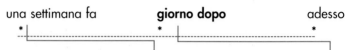

– Una settimana fa **avrei voluto** che il giorno dopo Rita **prendesse** un appuntamento con lo specialista.
(I would have liked Rita to make an appointment with the specialist a week ago.)

● the subordinate clause expresses contemporary time, i.e. the two actions happen at the *same time*, then the **imperfect subjunctive** is used:

ieri   adesso

– Mi **sarebbe piaciuto** che Diego mi **parlasse** del suo progetto di ricerca.
(I would have liked Diego to tell me about his research project.)

● the subordinate clause expresses an *earlier* time, i.e. the action in the subordinate clause happened *first*, then the **past perfect subjunctive** is used:

1990   1991   adesso

– **Avrei voluto** che l'anno precedente vi **foste iscritti** all'università.
(I would have liked you to have enrolled at University the previous year.)

hypothetical clauses

(se tu mangerai, io..., ecc.) (if you eat, I'll..., ecc.)

74

■ Study the examples. Which sentences express a probable hypothesis? Which one expresses an improbable hypothesis, which cannot be fulfilled because it refers to the past?

– Se mia madre mi **inviterà**, **andrò** da lei a pranzo domenica.
(If my mother invites me, I'll go there for lunch on Sunday.)

– Se **avessi** più tempo libero, **andrei** a trovare tutti i miei vecchi amici.
(If I had more free time, I would go and see all my old friends.)

– Se **fossi stato** meno pigro e avessi imparato qualche sport, non **sarei diventato** così grasso.
(If I hadn't been so lazy and had learnt to do some kind of sport, I wouldn't have got so fat.)

■ The hypothetical clause of **reality**

Probable condition: **se (if) + present or future indicative**	*Consequence:* **present or future indicative, or imperative**
Se avrò abbastanza soldi, *(If I have enough money,*	andrò in vacanza alle Maldive. *I'll go to the Maldives on holiday.)*
Se vieni a teatro stasera, *(If you come to the theatre this evening,*	dopo lo spettacolo ti invito a bere qualcosa. *I'll buy you a drink after the show.)*
Se chiami tua nonna, *(if you call your Grandmother,*	salutamela! *give her my regards)*

■ The hypothetical clause of **possibility**

Improbable condition, although theoretically possible **se + imperfect subjuncitve**	*Consequence in the present or future:* **conditional**
Se avessi abbastanza soldi, *(If I had enough money,*	andrei in vacanza alle Maldive. *I would go to the Maldives on holiday.)*
Se venissi a teatro stasera, *(If you came to the theatre this evening,*	dopo lo spettacolo ti inviterei a bere qualcosa. *I would buy you a drink after the show.*

■ The hypothetical clause of **impossibility**

Condition which was not fulfilled in the past: se + past perfect subjunctive	Consequence in the past: **perfect conditional**
Se avessi avuto abbastanza soldi, (If I had had enough money,	sarei andato in vacanza alle Maldive. I would have gone to the Maldives on holiday.)
Se fossi venuta a teatro ieri sera, (If you had come to the theatre yesterday evening,	dopo lo spettacolo ti avrei invitata a bere qualcosa. I would have bought you a drink after the show.)

Condition which was not fulfilled in the past: se + past perfect subjunctive	Consequence in the past: conditional
Se avessi guadagnato abbastanza soldi, (If I had earned enough money,	ora andrei in vacanza alle Maldive. I would go to the Maldives on holiday now.)
Se avessi preso qualche antibiotico, (If I had taken some antibiotics,	ora non avrei più la febbre. I wouldn't have a temperature now.)

▶ In spoken Italian the structure **se + imperfect indicative + imperfect indicative** is often used instead of **se + past perfect subjunctive + perfect conditional**:

Se **avevo** abbastanza soldi,	**andavo** in vacanza alle Maldive.
Se **venivi** a teatro ieri sera,	dopo lo spettacolo ti **invitavo** a bere qualcosa.

▶ the order of clauses can be inverted, with the if-clause coming after the main clause:

Avrei fatto un po' di ginnastica ieri sera, (I would have done some exercise yesterday evening,	se non avesse fatto tanto freddo. if it hadn't been so cold.)
Ti inviterò a cena, (I'll invite you to dinner,	se mi farai vedere le tue diapositive del Portogallo. if you show me your slides of Portugal.)

the passive (1)

(sono stato aiutato, ecc.) (I have been/was helped, etc.)

75

■ Study the example.

– Questa mattina l'agenzia 7 della
Cassa di Risparmio **è stata rapinata**
da tre uomini armati e mascherati.
*(This morning the number 7 branch of
the Cassa di Risparmio was robbed by
three armed men, wearing masks.)*

■ The **passive** is formed with the auxiliary *essere* in the various
tenses plus the *past participle* of the verb.

● Indicative

	active	passive
present	ascolto	**sono ascoltato**
passato prossimo	ho ascoltato	**sono stato ascoltato**
imperfect	ascoltavo	**ero ascoltato**
passato remoto	ascoltai	**fui ascoltato**
past perfect	avevo ascoltato	**ero stato ascoltato**
trapassato remoto	ebbi ascoltato	*non si usa*
simple future	ascolterò	**sarò ascoltato**
future perfect	avrò ascoltato	**sarò stato ascoltato**

● Subjunctive

	active	passive
present	che io ascolti	che *io* **sia ascoltato**
past	che io abbia ascoltato	che *io* **sia stato ascoltato**
imperfect	che io ascoltassi	che *io* **fossi ascoltato**
past perfect	che io avessi ascoltato	che *io* **fossi stato ascoltato**

● Conditional

	active	passive
present	ascolterei	**sarei ascoltato**
perfect	avrei ascoltato	**sarei stato ascoltato**

■ The **passive** can only be formed with **transitive** verbs:
  – Il bimbo **è stato morso** da un cane randagio.
  (The little boy was bitten by a stray dog.)

  Do you remember what *transitive verb* means?
  See Appendix 3.

■ The person or thing that performs the action (i.e. agent
  or instrument) is introduced by the preposition **da** *(by)*:
  – Parma **fu fondata dai** Romani.
  (Parma was founded by the Romans.)

▶ For the agreement of the past participle with the verb **essere**
  see, Unità 31.

(il giornale viene letto, ecc.) (the newspaper is/gets read, etc.)

■ Changing a verb from **active** to **passive**

active: Molti lettori	**hanno apprezzato**	*Il Nome della Rosa.*
(Many readers	*appreciated*	*Il Nome della Rosa.)*
passive: *Il Nome della Rosa*	**è stato apprezzato**	**da** molti lettori.
(Il Nome della Rosa	*was appreciated*	*by many readers.)*

► When the subject in the active is not defined (*loro* as in the following example, or *qualcuno*, etc.), the agent is **not** expressed il complemento d'agente (*da loro*, *da qualcuno*, etc.):

– Hanno perso un mazzo di chiavi   *(They have lost a bunch of keys.)*

– È stato perso un mazzo di chiavi.   *(A bunch of keys has been lost.)*

■ Questions with **chi** *(who)*?

ACTIVE: **Chi** ha scritto Il Nome della Rosa? ➙ *Il Nome della Rosa is the object.*
     (Who wrote Il Nome della Rosa?)

PASSIVE: **Da chi** è stato scritto Il Nome della Rosa? ➙ *Il Nome della Rosa is the subject.*
     (Who was Il Nome della Rosa written by?)

■ The passive with the **gerund**:
– La ricerca sul cancro sta facendo enormi progressi, **essendo** ora **finanziata** con nuovi fondi.
(Cancer Research is making great progress, now that it is being financed with new funds.)

■ The passive with the **infinitive**:
– Non piace a nessuno **essere deriso**.
(No one likes being mocked.)

■ Apart from the verb essere, the passive can also be formed with the verbs **venire** and **andare**, in the simple but not perfect tenses.

- The passive with **venire**:
  - La squadra argentina di calcio **veniva indicata** come la favorita del torneo.
  - La squadra argentina di calcio era indicata come la favorita del torneo.
    (The Argentinian team was considered favourite in the tournament.)
  - L'inglese **viene** oggi **studiato** nella maggior parte dei paesi.
  - L'inglese **è** oggi **studiato** nella maggior parte dei paesi.
    (English is studied in most countries nowadays.)

▶ The forms with **essere** and **venire** normally have the same meaning.

- The passive with **andare**.
  The passive with **andare** in most cases means **dovere** *(must, have to)*:
  - L'ultimo film di Bernardo Bertolucci **va visto** appena esce; dicono che sia un capolavoro.
  - L'ultimo film di Bernardo Bertolucci **deve essere visto** appena esce; dicono che sia un capolavoro.
    (It's a must to go and see Bernardo Bertolucci's latest film as soon as it comes out; they say it's a masterpiece.)
  - Il divieto di fumare **andrebbe esteso** a tutti i locali pubblici.
  - Il divieto di fumare **dovrebbe essere esteso** a tutti i locali pubblici.
    (The no-smoking law should be extended to all public places.)

▶ In some cases **andare** does not express obligation:
  - Nei roghi dell'Inquisizione andarono perduti libri di inestimabile valore.
    (Invaluable books were lost in the fires of the Inquisition.)

When it does not express obligation **andare** can also be used in perfect tenses:
  - Durante la notte alcune case **sono andate** parzialmente **distrutte** a causa di un'improvvisa tromba d'aria.
    (Some houses were partially destroyed during the night by an unexpected tornado.)

passive structures with si
(a Firenze si insegna l'italiano, ecc.)
(Italian is taught in Florence, etc.)

77

■ Study the picture.

Do you remember what a transitive
verb is? See Appendix 3.

SI AFFITTA
APPARTAMENTO
CON GARAGE
Tel. 0349 55 17 19

■ Instead of using the passive
structures with *essere, venire* or
andare, it is possible to use the
structure with **si** + the active voice
of the verb, but only with transitive verbs where the object is
expressed:

– A Firenze **si insegna** l'italiano a stranieri in molte scuole.
– (A Firenze l'italiano a stranieri **è/viene insegnato** in molte
scuole.)
(Italian is taught to foreigners in many schools in Florence.)

– Sull'Appennino **si trovano** molti funghi in autunno.
– (Sull'Appennino **vengono trovati** molti funghi in autunno.)
(You can find a lot of mushrooms in the Apennines in autumn.)

■ In the passive structure with **si** the verb is in the third person
singular if the noun it refers to is singular (1), or in the third
person plural if the noun it refers to is plural (2).
The verb is in the tense required by the meaning of the sentence:

– (1) Fino a pochi decenni fa in Italia **si parlava** soprattutto **il
dialetto**.
– (Fino a pochi decenni fa in Italia **era parlato** soprattutto **il
dialetto**.)
(Until a few decades ago mostly dialect was spoken in Italy.)

– (2) In Italia **si spendono molti soldi** per costruire nuove
autostrade.

- (In Italia **vengono spesi molti soldi** per costruire nuove autostrade.)
  (In Italy a lot of money is spent on building new motorways.)

■ In the perfect tenses the auxiliary is *essere* and the past participle agrees in gender and number with the noun it refers to:

- L'anno scorso **si sono registrat*i* tassi** d'interesse in leggero calo.
  (A slight drop in interest rates was registered last year.)

- **Si sono viste cose** interessantissime durante l'ultimo Festival di Spoleto.
  (There were some very interesting things to see during the last festival in Spoleto.)

▶ For the use of the **impersonal si**, see Unità 78.

impersonal si

78

(si mangia molto qui, ecc.) (You eat a lot here, etc.)

■ Impersonal si

Study the following sentences and consider the differences:
- In Toscana **si beve** del buon vino.
  (You can drink good wine in Tuscany.)
- In Italia **si beve** molto a tavola.
  (People drink a lot at meal times in Italy.)

In the first case there is a **passive structure with si**, because the verb is transitive *(beve)* and the object is expressed *(buon vino)*. In the second case it is an **impersonal si**; the verb is transitive *(beve)*, but the object is not expressed.

● With the **impersonal si** the verb is always in the **third person singular**.
  - In Spagna **si mangia** bene e non **si spende** molto.
    (You eat well and don't spend much in Spain.)

The verb can be *transitive*, with no object expressed, or *intransitive*:
  - In estate **si va** spesso in piscina per rinfrescarsi un po' $\longrightarrow$ *intransitive*
    (People often go to the swimming pool in summer to cool down a little.)
  - Se **si desidera** comunicare, **si parla**, ma **si deve** anche **ascoltare**. $\longrightarrow$ *all transitive*
    (If you want to communicate you need to speak, but you have to listen, too.)

● The **impersonal si** is sometimes used instead of the subject **noi** *(we)*:
  - **Si è pensato** di andare in montagna domani. $\longrightarrow$ **(Noi) abbiamo pensato** di andare in montagna domani.
    (We were thinking about going to the mountains tomorrow.)

■ Study the following sentences and consider the differences:
  – **Si è partiti tardi** e si è perso il traghetto per la Sardegna.
  – (**Noi siamo partiti** tardi e abbiamo perso il traghetto per la Sardegna).
  (We left late and missed our connection for Sardinia.)

  – **Si è mangiato** molto bene nella trattoria che ci hai consigliato.
  – (**Abbiamo mangiato** molto bene nella trattoria che ci hai consigliato).
  (We ate really well in the trattoria you recommended.)

The auxiliary in the compound tenses is *essere*, but only the past participle of verbs which have *essere* as an auxiliary in the active form agrees with the subject.

■ The **impersonal si** with *reflexive* or *pronominal* verbs.
In impersonal sentences with **si**, the **si** particle of the reflexive verb becomes **ci**:
  – **Ci si alza** più tardi quando si è in vacanza.
  (People get up later when they are on holiday.)
  – **Ci si incontra** spesso in birreria al sabato sera.
  (We often meet up in the pub on Saturday evenings.)

▶ The *past participle* in compound tenses is in the *plural masculine* form:
  – **Ci si è visti** varie volte e ci si saluta, ma non conosco il suo nome.
  (We have often seen and said hello to each other, but I don't know his/her name.)

■ The **impersonal si** with the verb *essere + adjective*.
In sentences with the verb *essere + si*, the adjective is always in the plural masculine form:
  – Quando **si è stanchi**, sarebbe meglio non uscire di sera.
  (When you are tired, it is better not to go out in the evening.)
  – **Si è felici** quando si ama.
  (People are happy when they are in love.)

■ **Loro** *(they)*

The structure with the third person plural **loro** is often used instead of the structure with the impersonal **si**.
The subject **loro** is often not expressed:

– **Hanno** cambiato il nome della via in cui abito.
(They have changed the name of the street where I live.)
– **Dicono** che in centro aprirà presto una nuova gelateria.
(They say a new ice-cream shop will soon be opening in the centre.)

■ **Uno** *(one)*

The pronoun **uno** *(one)* can also be used for the impersonal form. The verb is in the third person singular:

– **Uno** può viaggiare moltissimo, ma se non impara le lingue, si troverà sempre in difficoltà.
(You can travel a lot, but if you don't learn languages you will always have problems.)
– Se **uno** prende una multa, cosa deve fare?
(What do you have to do if you get a fine?)

■ **Tu** *(you)*

The impersonal form is sometimes expressed with the pronoun **tu** *(you)*. The verb is therefore in the second person singular.
The subject **tu** is often not expressed:

– Se **vai** a Perugia, **trovi** sempre tanti giovani di paesi lontani.
(If you go to Perugia you always meet lots of young people from foreign countries.)
– In montagna **devi** fare attenzione alle vipere.
(In the mountains you have to watch out for snakes.)

In these examples the subject **tu** indicates anyone.

▶ For the **impersonal si** see Unità 78.

80

trapassato remoto

(ebbi mangiato, fosti andato) (I had eaten, you had gone, etc.)

fui fosti fu	partito/a	ebbi avesti ebbe	mangiato
fummo foste furono	partiti/e	avemmo aveste ebbero	mangiato

■ **The trapassato remoto** is formed with the *passato remoto* of the auxiliaries *essere* or *avere* and the *past participle* of the verb:

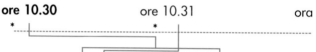

ore 10.30   ore 10.31   ora

   – **(Non) appena** il sindaco **ebbe terminato** il suo comizio, la
   gente **cominciò** a lasciare la piazza.
   (As soon as the mayor finished his speech the people
   started to leave the square.)

■ The **trapassato remoto** is used to talk about an action which took place *just* before another event expressed in the *passato remoto*.

▶ It is only used in subordinate time clauses and it follows conjunctions like **dopo che** *(after)*, **quando** *(when)*, **(non) appena** *(no sooner than, as soon as)*.
   – **Dopo che** Lisa **ebbe appreso** la notizia della partenza di
   Tommaso, **corse** a casa di Giuseppe.
   (After she had heard about Tommaso leaving, Lisa ran to
   Giuseppe's house.)

▶ The *trapassato prossimo* is rarely used.

▶ See also Unità 48 - The past perfect.

reported speech (1)
(lui dice che ha mangiato tutto, ecc.)
(he says he has eaten/ate everything, etc.)

81

■ Study the picture.
There are two ways of telling
someone something. Directly:
"Ci vediamo a casa sua alle 8".
Or with reported/indirect speech,
i.e. reporting what someone else
said: *Anna dice che vi vedete a
casa tua alle 8.*

> Ci vediamo a casa sua alle 8.

> Anna dice che vi vedete a casa tua alle 8.

■ When transforming direct speech into reported speech it is
necessary to change different elements in the sentence, for
example subject, verb (tense and form), personal pronouns,
possessive adjectives, time and place expressions, etc.

■ **Changes in tenses starting from the past**
When reporting something that was said/thought/believed, etc.
in the past, the verb in the main clause is in the *passato prossimo/remoto* or *imperfect: disse, ha detto, diceva*, etc.:

direct speech	reported speech
Present Grazia **disse**: "**Devo** andare a casa." *(Grazia said: "I have to go home".)*	*Imperfect* Grazia **disse** che **doveva** andare a casa. *(Grazia said: that she had to go home.)*
Passato prossimo Grazia **disse: "Sono arrivata** a casa tardi." *(Grazia said: "I arrived home late".)*	*Past perfect* Grazie **disse** che **era arrivata** a casa tardi. *(Grazia said that she had got home late.)*
Passato remoto Grazia **disse**: "Da piccola **volli** imparare a giocare a tennis. *(Grazia said:"When I was a child I wanted to learn to play tennis.)*	*Past perfect* Grazia **disse** che da piccola **aveva voluto** imparare a giocare a tennis. *(Grazia said that when she was a child she had wanted to learn to play tennis.)*

direct speech	reported speech
Future Quando aveva dieci anni Grazia **disse**: "Da grande **imparerò** a giocare a tennis." *(When she was 10 Grazia said: "When I'm older I'll learn to play tennis.")*	*Perfect conditional* Quando aveva dieci anni Grazia **disse** che da grande **avrebbe imparato** a giocare a tennis. *(When she was 10 Grazia said that when she was older she would learn to play tennis.)*

➤ Study the time line and the example:

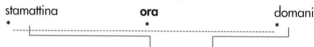

stamattina   **ora**   domani

– Sonia stamattina mi **ha detto**: "**Tornerò** domani."
– Sonia stamattina mi **ha detto** che **tornerà** domani.

If the action expressed in reported speech has not taken place yet, i.e. it is still a future event, the verb remains in the future.

■ Changes in tenses starting from the present
When reporting something that is said/thought/believed, etc. in the present or future, the verb in the main clause is in the present or future: *dice, dirà,* etc.
When transforming direct speech into reported speech, tenses do not change:

direct speech	reported speech
Presente Grazia **dice**: "Gli Stati Uniti **sono** lontani." *(Grazia says: "The U.S.A. is far away".)*	*Presente* Grazie **dice** che gli Stati Uniti **sono** lontani. *(Grazia says that the U.S.A. is far away.)*
Passato prossimo Quando vedrò Grazia mi **dirà**: "**Sono stata** in pizzeria ieri sera." *(When I see Grazia, she'll say: "I went to a pizzeria yesterday evening.")*	*Passato prossimo* Quando la vedrò Grazia mi **dirà** che **è stata** in pizzeria ieri sera. *(When I see Grazia, she'll tell me that she went to a pizzeria yesterday evening.)*

reported speech (2)
(lui crede che io vada..., ecc.) (he thinks I'm going..., etc.)

82

■ **Changes in form: from the indicative to the subjunctive**

Osserva e analizza gli esempi.

Giovanni **chiese**: "Paul **è** inglese?" ⟶ Giovanni chiese se
Paul **fosse** inglese.

(Giovanni asked: "Is Paul English?") *Giovanni asked if Paul*
were English.)

Paola **chiede**: "Tua sorella ⟶ Paola **chiede** se sua
si **chiama** Alba?" sorella si **chiami** Alba.
(Paola asks: "Is your sister's *Paola is asking if her/his*
name Alba?") *sister's name is Alba.)*

If the verb in the main clause takes the subjunctive, then the verb
in the subordinate clauses is in the subjunctive and the tense
changes are as shown in the table below.

■ **Changes in form and tense starting from the past**

direct speech	reported speech
Present Grazia **chiese**: "Luca **deve** andare a casa?" *(Grazia asked: "Does Luca have to go home?")*	*Imperfect* Grazia **chiese** se Luca **dovesse** andare a casa. *(Grazia asked if Luca had to go home.)*
Passato prossimo Grazia **chiese**: "Cristina, **sei arrivata** a casa tardi sabato sera?" *(Grazia asked: "Cristina, did you get home late on Saturday evening?")*	*Past Perfect* Grazia **chiese** se Cristina **fosse arrivata** a casa tardi sabato sera? *(Grazia asked if Cristina had got home late on Saturday evening.)*
Passato remoto Grazia **disse**: "Quante volte Colombo **arrivò** in America?" *(Grazia asked:"How many times did Columbus reach America?")*	*Past Perfect* Grazia **chiese** quante volte Colombo **fosse arrivato** in America. *(Grazia asked how many times Columbus (had) reached America.)*
Future Quando aveva 10 anni Grazia **chiese**: "Da grande mi **insegnerete** a giocare a tennis?" *(When she was 10, Grazia asked: "When I'm older, will you teach me how to play tennis?")*	*Perfect Conditional* Quando aveva 10 anni Grazia **chiese** se da grande le **avrebbero insegnato** a giocare a tennis. *(When she was 10, Grazia asked if they would teach her how to play tennis when she was older.)*

■ Tense changes are the same as for the indicative. Only the form changes, because in this case the subjunctive is used.

Study the example.
– Karl **dice**: "L'italiano **è** difficile." ➞ Karl **crede** che l'italiano
  (Karl says: "Italian is difficult.")   **sia** difficile.
                                            *(Karl thinks that Italian
                                            is difficult.)*

When changing from direct speech to reported speech other verbs can be used instead of *dire (say)*, for example: *credere, pensare, ritenere (believe, think, consider)*, which take the subjunctive.

▶ *Chiedere (ask)* can be followed either by the subjunctive or the indicative.

■ **Changes in form and tense starting from the present**

Sometimes when transforming direct speech into reported speech the tenses do not change, but the form does:

direct speech	reported speech
Present Grazia **chiede**: "Venezia **è** vicino a Padova?" *(Grazia asks: "Is Venice near Padua?")*	*Present* Grazia **chiede** se Venezia **sia** vicino a Padova. *(Grazia asks if Venice is near Padua.)*

■ **Changes in form: from the imperative to the subjunctive**

direct speech	reported speech
Starting from the past *Imperative* Grazia **disse**: "**Andatevene!**" *(Grazia said:"Go away!")*	*Imperfect subjunctive* Grazia **ordinò** che se ne **andassero**. *(Grazia ordered them to leave.)*
Starting from the present *Imperative* Grazia **dice**: "**Andatevene!**" *(Grazia says: "Go away!")*	*Present subjunctive* Grazia **ordina** che se ne **vadano**. *(Grazia orders them to leave.)*

▶ In the two examples above the structure (**di + infinitive**) can be used instead of the subjunctive:
Grazia disse: "Andatevene!" ➞ Grazia ordinò loro **di andarsene**.
Grazia dice: "Andatevene!" ➞ Grazia ordina loro **di andarsene**.

reported speech (3)
(lui dice che quella è la sua casa, ecc.)
(he says (that), that is his house, etc.)

83

■ **Changes in subjects, personal pronouns and possessives**
Study the following examples.

– "Ciao, ragazzi. **Vi** telefon**o** più tardi!" ⟶
  ("Bye. I'll ring you later.")
  Sandro saluta gli amici, dicendo che telefon**a loro** più tardi.
  *Sandro is says goodbye to his friends and promises to
  ring them later.*
– "Lucia, **vai** da **tua** madre stasera?" ⟶
  ("Lucia, are you going to your mother's this evening?")
  Sandro chiede a Lucia se **va** da **sua** madre stasera.
  Sandro asks Lucia if she is going to her mother's this evening.

When transforming direct speech into reported speech, subject and
object personal pronouns, possessives and verbs all change. If the
subject in the main clause is in the third person singular or plural
(*lui, lei, loro*), as in the examples above (*Sandro dice..., Sandro
chiede...*), pronouns, adjectives and verbs in the first and second
person singular (*io, tu*) and plural (*noi, voi*) change to the third
person (singular and plural):

– "Lucia, **dobbiamo** andare al mercato domattina o **ti sei**
  messa d'accordo con i **nostri** amici?"
  ("Lucia, do we have to go to the market tomorrow morning
  or have you arranged something with our friends?")
⟶ Sandro chiede a Lucia se domattina **devono** andare al
  mercato o se **si è** messa d'accordo con i **loro** amici.
  *(Sandro asks Lucia if they have to go to the market tomorrow
  morning or if she has arranged something with their friends.)*

■ **Changes in expressions of time**
Study the examples.
– **Oggi** sono contento perché ho superato l'esame di filologia.
  (I'm happy today because I've passed my philology exam.)
⟶ Davide disse che **quel giorno** era contento perché aveva
  superato l'esame di filologia.

(Davide said he was happy that day because he had passed his philology exam.)
– **Domani** farò una festa con tutti i miei amici.
(I'm going to have a party with all my friends tomorrow.)
➤ Davide disse che **il giorno dopo** avrebbe fatto una festa con tutti i suoi amici.
(Davide said he would have a party with all his friends the following day.)

direct speech	reported speech
oggi *(today)*	quel giorno *(that day)*
domani *(tomorrow)*	il giorno seguente/successivo il giorno dopo *(the following/next day)*
fra una settimana *(in a week)*	la settimana dopo/la settimana seguente/successiva *(the following week)*
stamattina questo pomeriggio (ecc.) *(this morning, this afternoon, etc.)*	quella mattina quel pomeriggio (ecc.) *(that morning, that afternoon)*
ieri, ieri sera *(yesterday, yesterday evening)*	il giorno precedente, il giorno prima, la sera prima *(the previous day, the previous evening)*
un'ora fa, tre giorni fa un mese fa, il mese scorso, ora/adesso *(an hour ago, three days ago, a month ago, now)*	un'ora prima, tre giorni prima, un mese prima , il mese prima/precedente, allora/in quel momento *(an hour earlier, three days before, a month before, the previous month, then/at the time)*

■ Changes in expressions of place

Qui, qua *(here)* ➞ **lì, là** *(there)*
– "Non muoverti da **qui**!" ➞ Sandro ordinò a suo figlio di non muoversi da **lì**.

("Don't move from here!" *Sandro ordered his son not to move from there.)*

■ Changes in demonstratives

Questo/a/i/e *(this/these)* ➞ **quel/quella**/ecc. *(that/those)*

– "Non ho mai letto **questo** libro." ➞ Sandro disse che non aveva mai letto quel libro.

("I have never read this book." *Sandro said he had never read that book.)*

■ Andare ➞ venire *(go ➞ come)*

– Sandro mi disse: "vuoi **venire** al cinema con me?".
 (Sandro said: do you want to come to the cinema with me?")
– Sandro mi disse se volevo **andare** al cinema con lui.
 (Sandro asked me if I wanted to go to the cinema with him.)

■ **Present infinitive:** form

present	past
andare *(to go)*	**essere andato** *(to have gone)*

■ **Present infinitive:** use
Study the examples.

– **Fare** ginnastica fa bene alla salute.
(Doing gymnastics is good for your health.)
– Devi **dire** a tuo fratello di **venirmi** a **trovare**.
(You must tell your brother to come and see me.)

In the examples above there are various infinitives. In the first example the infinitive acts as a noun; it is also possible to say: la ginnastica fa bene alla salute, *(Gymnastics is good for your health)*; in the second example, the three infinitives act as verbs.

● When it acts as a **noun** the **infinitive** is the **subject** of the clause:

– **Abitare** in campagna è bello.
(Living in the country is nice.)

Sometimes the article **il, lo, l'** can be placed before the infinitive:

– **Il parlare** male di una persona in sua assenza non è corretto.
(It is not nice to talk about someone behind their back.)

● When it acts like a verb it can be independent (especially as an imperative, both negative and affirmative):
  – Non **gettare** oggetti dal finestrino.
   (Don't throw things out of the window.)

Or it can depend on another verb (with or without a preposition before it):
  – Mi piace **nuotare**. *(I like swimming.)*

■ **Verbs with the infinitive without preposition**

Dovere, potere, sapere, volere *(must, can, know, want)*	Devi **andare** a letto presto, se vuoi **stare** bene al mattino. *(You have to go to bed early if you want to feel good in the morning.)*
lasciare, fare *(let, make)*	Lascia **perdere**, è meglio! *(Forget it, it's better.)*
ascoltare, guardare, sentire, vedere, osservare, ecc. *(listen, look, hear, see, watch, etc.)*	Ti ascolto **suonare** la chitarra e mi ricordo quando ero giovane. *(Listening to you playing the guitar, reminds me of when I was young.)*
piacere, desiderare, preferire *(like, would like, prefer)*	Desidero **finire** questo lavoro al più presto. *(I'd like to finish this job as soon as possible.)*
basta, bisogna, occorre *(be enough, need, be necessary)*	Bisogna **aspettare** un momento. *(We have to wait a bit)*
essere + aggettivo, avverbio *(be + adjective, adverb)*	Spesso è inutile **piangere**, è meglio **affrontare** i problemi. *(It's pointless crying; it's better to face up to problems.)*
osare *(dare)*	Non oso **disturbarla** quando dorme. *(I wouldn't dare disturb her when she's asleep.)*

84

With *volere, desiderare, piacere* and *preferire (want, would like, like and prefer)* the structure with the infinitive cannot be used if the subject of the subordinate clause is different from the one in the main clause.

- **(Io) Preferisco** che **tu** venga da me domani.
  (I'd rather you came to see me tomorrow.)
- **(Io) Vorrei** che **lei** fosse sempre con me.
  (I wish she were always with me.)

▶ The *unstressed personal pronouns, ne* and *ci* follow the infinitive and the final vowel of the verb is dropped.
See Unità 40.

parlar**e** + **gli**   parlar**gli**   discuter**e** + **ne**   discuter**ne**

The verb **sapere** *(know)* is used without the preposition **di** when it means *essere capace (be able to)*.

So **nuotare**	but	So **di** non essere un bravo cuoco.
=		=
– Sono capace di nuotare.		Mi rendo conto di non essere un bravo cuoco.
(I can swim.)		*(I know I'm not a good cook.)*

verbs/adjectives + *di* + infinitive

85

(spero di andare, ecc.) (I hope to go, etc.)

■ The most frequent verbs followed by preposition
di + infinitive listed in alphabetical order

*affermare * (maintain)*	L'imputato afferma di essere innocente.
*ammettere * (admit)*	L'imputato ha ammesso di essere colpevole.
avere bisogno (need)	I Rossi hanno bisogno di trovare un nuovo appartamento.
avere il diritto/dovere (be one's right/duty)	Ogni italiano ha il dovere di rispettare le leggi.
avere paura (be afraid of)	Ho paura di fare un incidente in moto.
avere tempo (have time)	Silvia non ha tempo di fare la traduzione.
avere voglia (to feel like)	Ho sempre voglia di dormire.
cercare (try)	Cerco sempre di fare del mio meglio.
chiedere (ask)	Gli ho chiesto di farmi un favore.
*credere * (believe, think)*	Credo di essere abbastanza fortunato nella vita.
*decidere * (decide)*	Abbiamo deciso di tornare in Francia.
*dimenticare/si * (forget)*	Mi sono dimenticato di fare la spesa.
dire (say, tell)	Ho detto alla donna di servizio di non cucinare più.
*dubitare * (doubt)*	Dubito di arrivare in tempo.
*evitare * (avoid)*	Bisogna evitare di mettersi nei guai.
finire (finish)	Ho finito di lavorare in tempo per prendere l'autobus.
*immaginare * (imagine)*	Immagino spesso di essere su una spiaggia deserta.
impedire (prevent, forbid)	Ti impedisco di entrare in casa mia.
*lamentarsi * (complain)*	Ci lamentiamo sempre di vivere dove c'è nebbia.
*negare * (deny)*	Nego di essere io il colpevole.
ordinare (order)	Gli ho ordinato di finire il lavoro prima di sera.
*pensare * (think)*	Penso di essere un calciatore molto mediocre.
permettere (allow)	Il dottore non mi permette di bere alcolici.
pregare (pray)	Prega di non incontrarlo per strada.
proibire (forbid, not allow)	Mi hanno proibito di fumare.
ricordarsi (remember)*	Non mi ricordo mai di telefonare a Carlo.
ritenere (think)*	Ritengo di poter andare in Cina presto.
sforzarsi (try hard)	Lui si sforza di essere simpatico, ma non ci riesce.
smettere (give up)	Ho smesso di fumare.
sognare (dream)*	Sogno di diventare un grande ballerino.

sperare* (hope)	Spero di andare in pensione presto.
supporre * (suppose)	Supponiamo di poter partire subito. Dove andresti?
temere * (to be afraid)	Teme di non poter aver figli.
tentare (try)	Ha tentato di battere il proprio record nei 100 metri.
terminare (finish, stop)	Terminiamo spesso di lavorare alle 8.
tollerare * (can't stand)	Non tollero di dovere svegliarmi sempre alle 7.
vergognarsi * (be ashamed)	Mi vergogno di non sapere una parola di arabo.
vietare (forbid)	Mia moglie mi ha vietato di parlare con la mia ex.

▶ The verbs marked with the asterisk * are followed by the preposition **di** if the subject of the main clause is the same as the subject in the subordinate clause:

   – Penso **di** essere felice.   (I think I'm happy.)
   – Penso **che tu** sia felice.   (I think you're happy.)

■ Some adjectives are followed by the preposition **di + infinitive**

capace (able)	Non sono capace di cantare.
contento (pleased)	Sono contento di fare il bagno nel mare di Capri.
convinto (sure)	Sei convinta di essere una brava attrice?
curioso (curious)	Sono curioso di leggere il tuo nuovo libro.
felice (happy)	Sono felice di stare in vacanza.
libero (free)	Sono libero di andare dove voglio.
orgoglioso (proud)	È orgoglioso di essere italiano.
sicuro (sure)	Sei sicuro di dire la verità?
stanco (tired)	Lino è stanco di lavorare.

(non riesco a mangiare, ecc.) (I can't eat, etc.)

■ Study the pictures.

*Posso **aiutarla** a portare la valigia?*

*Fermiamoci un momento; non sono **abituato** a correre tanto!*

■ The most frequent verbs followed by the proposition **a + infinitive** listed in alphabetical order

abituarsi (get used to)	È difficile abituarsi a mangiare sempre pasta.
accompagnare (accompany, go with)	Mi accompagni a far spesa?
andare (go)	Elena va a prendere la bimba all'asilo.
annoiarsi (get bored)	Teresa, l'ascensorista, non si annoia a far sempre gli stessi movimenti.
arrivare (arrive, get to)	Siamo arrivati a comprare il latte quando il negozio stava chiudendo.
aiutare (help)	Ti aiuto a finire i compiti?
cominciare (start, take up)	Ho cominciato a correre ogni giorno.
continuare (continue, keep on)	Voglio continuare a fare ginnastica con costanza.
convincere (convince)	Ho convinto mia moglie a correre con me.
correre (run)	Dopo due ore di ginnastica sono corso a dormire; ero stanco morto.
divertirsi (enjoy oneself)	I giovani si divertono a stare in discoteca fino alle 5 del mattino.
entrare (go in)	Il giovane è entrato nell'ufficio a parlare con il direttore.
fare in tempo (make it/do something in time)	Non ho fatto in tempo a scrivere una lettera a Andrea.

imparare (learn)	Non ho ancora imparato a giocare a tennis.
incoraggiare (encourage)	Sua moglie lo incoraggia spesso a ballare, ma lui non ne vuole sapere.
iniziare (start)	Ho iniziato a studiare l'inglese a 14 anni.
insegnare (teach)	Mi hanno insegnato a pronunciare l'inglese con un metodo efficace.
invitare (invite)	Ti invito a bere una birra; ci vieni?
mandare (send)	Ho mandato mio fratello in posta a spedire una raccomandata.
mettersi (get down to)	Se mi mettessi a studiare con questo caldo, non capirei niente.
portare (lead to)	Il troppo esercizio fisico mi ha portato a mangiare il triplo.
prepararsi (get ready)	La signora si preparò a ricevere gli ospiti.
provare (try)	Ho provato a telefonarti ma non eri a casa.
restare (stay)	Stasera resto a giocare a carte con gli amici fino alle 11.
rinunciare (give up)	Ho rinunciato a imparare a ballare, dopo inutili tentativi.
riuscire (manage)	Sono riuscito a trovare il tuo numero di telefono sull'elenco.
spingere (push)	La tragedia che lo ha colpito lo ha spinto a suicidarsi.
stare (stay)	Devo stare in ufficio fino a tardi a finire un lavoro.
tornare (go back)	Torno a prenderti alle 10.
venire (come)	Vengo a trovarti domenica pomeriggio.
volerci (take)	Ci vogliono 3 ore a finire questo lavoro.

■ Some adjectives are followed by the preposition **a + infinitive**

abile (clever, good)	Luca è molto abile a vendere cose inutili.
abituato (used to)	Sono abituato a svegliarmi presto.
attento (careful)	Stai attento a non sporcarti troppo.
interessato (interested)	Sono interessato a tutto quanto riguarda il Sud America.
lento (slow)	Mio nonno non era lento a capire le cose, anzi era
veloce (fast)	molto veloce a cogliere quanto poteva interessarlo.
occupato (busy)	Il direttore è occupato a controllare il lavoro degli operai.
pronto (prepared/ready)	Sono pronto a seguirti fino in capo al mondo.

da & per + infinitive 87

(un libro da leggere, ecc.) (a book to read, etc.)

DA   indicates purpose

with **c'è/ci sono** *(there is/are)*:

– A Firenze **ci sono** molte cose **da** vedere. → *(...cose che*
  (There are many things to see in Florence.)   *devono esse-*
                                                   re viste/che
                                                   vale la pena
                                                   vedere.)

– **C'è** ancora molto **da** fare per uscire dalla → *(Devono*
  crisi economica.   *essere fatte*
  (There is still a lot to do in order to   *molte*
  recover from the economic crisis.)   *cose/biso-*
                                                   gna fare.)

– Devono essere fatte molte cose/bisogna fare.
  (Many things must/have to/need to be done.)

● with **avere**, meaning *dovere (must/have to)*:
  – **Ho** molto **da** lavorare oggi. →*(Devo lavorare molto oggi.)*
                                            (I have to do a lot of work today.)

● with a **noun**, in expressions such as:
  – Un appartamento **da** affittare → *(Un appartamento libero*
    (A flat to let)   *che si può affittare.)*
  – Una macchina **da** cucire   → *(Una macchina che si*
    (A sewing machine)   *usa per cucire.)*

● with **qualcosa** *(something)*:
  – Vuoi **qualcosa da** leggere? → *(Do you want something*
                                 to read?)

  – Mio zio ha sempre **qualcosa** → *(My uncle always*
    da fare.   *has something to do.)*

Study the examples with **da** again. Is there a preposition with the same function in your language too?

> **PER + INFINITIVE** is used in clauses of purpose, i.e. it means **al fine di/allo scopo di** *(in order to)*:

– Mi sono alzato presto **per andare** in montagna.   ⟶ ...al fine di...
(I got up early to go to the mountains.)

– L'ho chiamato **per sapere** cosa è   ⟶ ...al fine di...
successo ieri sera.
(I called him to find out what happened yesterday evening.)

▶ This construction can only be used when the subject in the main clause is the same as the subject in the subordinate clause:

    IO   **IO**
– Le ho parlato **per spiegarle** cosa doveva fare.
(I spoke to her in order to explain what she had to do.)

    IO   **LEI**
– Le ho parlato **affinché lei mi spiegasse** cosa doveva fare.
(I spoke to her so that she would tell me what she had to do.)

For the use of *affinché (so that)*, see Unità 70.

▶ For the construction *stare per*, see Unità 53.

■ **Perfect infinitive**: form

present	perfect
essere	essere stato/a/i/e
avere	avere avuto
mangiare	aver mangiato
andare	essere andato/a/i/e
potere	aver potuto

The perfect infinitive is formed with the *present infinitive* of the verbs *essere* or *avere* + the *past participle* of the verb.

▶ In the perfect infinitive *aver* is used instead of the full word *avere*.

■ **Perfect infinitive**: use
Study the examples.

 – **Dopo aver speso** tutti i soldi, sono tornato a casa.
  (After having spent all my money I went back home)
 – Quando sono arrivato a casa, mi sono arrabbiato con me stesso **per** non **aver comprato** il latte.
  (When I got home I was really annoyed with myself for not having bought the milk.)

In the two examples above the perfect infinitive is used because the action in the subordinate clause took place before the event in the main clause.

■ The **perfect infinitive** is used with

DOPO *(after)*

Study the examples.

– **Dopo aver dormito** dodici ore ero ancora stanco.
   (I was still tired even after having slept for twelve hours.)

– **Dopo** che Luca **era arrivato** a casa, sua madre gli diede la
   buona notizia.
   (When Luca got home, his mother gave him the good news.)

What are the subjects of the two sentences above?

The phrase **dopo** + infinitive can only be used when the subject
of the main clause is the same as the subject of the subordinate
clause.

> **PER**   which introduces the cause of the event in the main
>   clause.

– La conosco **per aver studiato** insieme
   all'università   ⟶   *(implicit)*

– La conosco **perché abbiamo** studiato
   insieme all'università.   ⟶   *(explicit)*
   (I know her because we studied together at University.)

Even with **per**, the structure with the infinitive can only be used
when the subject of the main clause is the same as the subject of
the subordinate clause.

■ The infinitive is used in expressions, such as

PRIMA DI *(before)*

– **Prima di salire** sul treno abbracciai mia madre.
(I hugged my mother before getting on the train.)

The phrase **prima** + infinitive can only be used when the subject of the main clause is the same as the subject in the subordinate:

– Prima di mangiare mi sono lavato le mani.
(I washed my hands before eating.)
– Prima che mia moglie tornasse ho passato l'aspirapolvere.
(Before my wife came back I took the hoover over the room.)

SENZA *(without)*

– Sono partito per la Svezia **senza cambiare** i soldi.
(I left for Sweden without changing any money.)

The phrase **senza** + infinitive can only be used when the subject of the main clause is the same as the subject in the subordinate:

– Senza fumare sto molto meglio.
(I feel much better now that I don't smoke.)
– Le ho preso 5 euro senza che se ne accorgesse.
(I took 5 euro from her without her noticing.)

INVECE DI *(instead of)*

– **Invece di lamentarti**, cerca di risolvere il problema!
(Instead of complaining, try and solve the problem!)

Invece di is a synonym of *al posto di, anziché.*
The phrase **invece di** + infinitive can only be used when the subject of the main clause is the same as the subject in the subordinate clause.

A COSTO DI *(even if)*

– **A costo di inventarmi** tutto, gli dirò che va tutto bene.
– Anche se dovrò inventarmi tutto, gli dirò che va tutto bene.

(I'll tell him everything is going well even if I have to make it all up.)

The phrase **a costo di** + infinitive can only be used when the subject of the main clause is the same as the subject in the subordinate clause.

A FORZA DI *(by keeping on)*

– **A forza di ripetere** che in Italia si vive bene, se ne sta convincendo.
– Continuando a ripetere che in Italia si vive bene, se ne sta convincendo.
(By continually repeating that life in Italy is good, he is actually convincing himself)

The phrase **a forza di** + infinitive can only be used when the subject of the main clause is the same as the subject in the subordinate clause.

IN MODO DA *(so as to, in order to)*

– Ho scritto a mio fratello **in modo da raccontargli** ciò che è accaduto.
– Ho scritto a mio fratello, così posso raccontargli ciò che è accaduto.
(I have written to my brother, in order to tell him what has happened.)

The phrase **in modo da** + infinitive can only be used when the subject of the main clause is the same as the subject in the subordinate.

– Ho comprato una piccola barca in modo da poter visitare alcune spiaggette tranquille.
(I have bought a little boat in order to visit some nice quiet beaches.)
– Roberto ha detto tutta la verità a Stefania in modo che lei possa decidere liberamente che cosa fare.
(Roberto told Stefania the whole truth so that she can decide what to do.)

■ The **gerund** has two forms: *present gerund* and *past gerund*.

present gerund		past gerund
cant **-are**	cant **-ando**	**avendo cantato**
cred **-ere**	cred **-endo**	**avendo creduto**
sent **-ire**	sent **-endo**	**essendo andato/a/i/e**
fin **-ire**	fin **-endo**	**essendo partito/a/i/e**

■ Some irregular forms

bere	bev **-endo**
condurre	conduc **-endo**
dire	dic **-endo**
fare	fac **-endo**
porre	pon **-endo**
trarre	tra **-endo**

■ The **past gerund** is formed with the *present gerund* of the verbs *essere* or *avere* + the past participle of the verb.

■ The **gerund** can have different functions, indicating:

TIME

- **Giocando** a calcio bisogna osservare la posizione dei compagni.
- **Quando si gioca** a calcio bisogna osservare la posizione dei compagni.
  (When playing football you need to watch where the other team members are positioned.)

MEANS

- **Leggendo** si imparano tante cose. /**Con la lettura** si imparano tante cose. *(You learn lots of things by reading.)*

CAUSE

- **Essendomi divertito** molto alcuni anni fa, quest'anno sono tornato in Sardegna.

– **Poiché/dato che mi sono divertito** molto alcuni anni fa,
quest'anno sono tornato in Sardegna.
*(As I enjoyed myself so much a few years ago, I went back
to Sardinia this year.)*

HYPOTHESIS

– **Risparmiando** molto riusciresti a comprarti un
appartamento.
– **Se risparmiassi** molto, riusciresti a comprarti un
appartamento.
(If you saved hard you would be able to buy yourself a flat.)

CONCESSION used with **pur** *(although)*

– **Pur** non **avendo sonno** è andata a letto con il suo bimbo.
– **Anche se** non **aveva sonno**, è andata a letto con il suo bimbo.
(Although she wasn't tired, she went to bed with her son)

■ The **present gerund** is used when the action in the main
clause happens at the same time as the event in the
subordinate clause:

         ore 17   ora

⌐⌐⌐⌐⌐⌐⌐⌐⌐⌐⌐⌐⌐⌐⌐⌐⌐⌐⌐⌐⌐⌐⌐⌐⌐⌐⌐⌐⌐⌐⌐⌐⌐⌐⌐⌐⌐

– **Correndo** sono caduto.   *(I fell while I was running.)*

■ The **past gerund** is used when the action in the main clause
follows the event in the subordinate clause, i.e. the action expressed
by the past gerund happened at an earlier time in the past:

       ore 20   *ore 23*

⌐⌐⌐⌐⌐⌐⌐⌐⌐⌐⌐⌐⌐⌐⌐⌐⌐⌐⌐⌐⌐⌐⌐⌐⌐⌐⌐⌐⌐⌐⌐⌐⌐⌐

– **Avendo mangiato** troppo, ho dovuto prendere un bicchiere
d'acqua con un po' di bicarbonato.
*(Having eaten too much, I had to have a glass of water with
some baking soda.)*

■ The **gerund** is generally used when the subject in the main
clause is the same as the subject is the subordinate clause
(i.e. the sentence with the gerund).

▶ For the use of the **present gerund** with the verb *stare*, see Unità 52.
▶ The *unstressed personal pronouns*, *ci* and *ne* follow the
gerund; see Unità 40.

■ **Present participle**: form

present participle	
cant **-are**	cant **-ante**
cred **-ere**	cred **-ente**
segui-**ire**	segu **-ente**

■ Some irregular forms

present participle	
bere	bev **-ente**
condurre	conduc **-ente**
dire	dic **-ente**
fare	fac **-ente**
porre	pon **-ente**
trarre	tra **-ente**

Several verbs in -ire form the present participle in **-iente**.

ubbidi**re**   ⟶   ubbid**iente** *(obedient)*
conveni**re**   ⟶   conven**iente** *(wortwhile)*

■ **Present participle**: use

The **present participle** can be used as an *adjective*, a *noun* or a *verb*.

It is most frequently used as an adjective and as a noun.

ADJECTIVES   Some examples

una casa **accogliente**	*(a welcoming house)*
una donna **affascinante**	*(a fascinating woman)*
un incidente **terrificante**	*(a terrible accident)*
una borsa **pesante**	*(a heavy bag)*

NOUNS   Some examples

Il presidente	il/la commerciante	il/la partecipante
l'insegnante	il/la dipendente	il/la cantante
la corrente		

(the president, the shopkeeper, the participant, the teacher, the employee, the singer, the current)

As adjective and as noun the present participle ends in **e** in the *singular* form and in **i** in the *plural* form.

VERBS

When it is used as a verb the present participle acts as **relative clause** (che....).

In modern Italian this use is limited to bureaucratic language.

- I cittadini **residenti** in questo quartiere dovranno recarsi a votare al seggio 209.
- I cittadini **che risiedono** in questo quartiere dovranno recarsi a votare al seggio 209.
  (Residents in this area must vote at polling station 209.)

■ **Past participle**

For the *forms* of the past participle see Unità 31.

■ Other uses of the **past participle**:

As an **adjective**

- Con il segnale luminoso **acceso** non si può utilizzare la macchina.
  (The machine cannot be used when the light is on.)

As a **noun**

- Gli **ammalati** gravi devono essere ricoverati in ospedale.
  (Seriously ill people must be admitted to hospital.)

As a **verb**
For the use of the past participle in the *perfect tenses*, see the relevant units.

When it is used without an auxiliary, the past participle of transitive verbs has a *passive* meaning. It can replace a whole **relative** clause.

- La casa, **distrutta** dal terremoto, non fu ricostruita. =
- La casa, **che era stata distrutta** dal terremoto non fu ricostruita.
  (The house, destroyed by the earthquake, was not re-built.)

coordinate conjunctions (1)

(e, o, né...né, ecc.) (and, or, neither... nor, etc.)

92

■ **Coordinate conjunctions** are used to join two main clauses in a single sentence.

The two sentences become two main *coordinate* clauses.

E *(and)*

– La mia scuola è moderna **e** vi funzionano parecchi corsi.
  (My school is modern and many courses are run there.)

When it is followed by a word beginning in **e**, it normally becomes **ed**.

– La mia scuola è moderna **ed** efficiente.
  (My school is modern and efficient.)

O *(or)*

– In estate si può rimanere in città **o** si può evitare il caldo andando in montagna.
  (In the summer you can stay in town or you can get away from the heat by going to the mountains.)

O introduces an alternative to what is said in the first clause. Do you know any synonyms of **o**? See Unità 93.

MA *(but)*

– Quando andavo a scuola sapevo che la fisica era importante, **ma** non mi piaceva.
  (When I went to school I knew that physics was important, but I didn't like it.)

Do you know any synonyms of **ma**? See Unità 93.

ANCHE *(also, too)*

It is used in *affirmative* sentences. It can occupy different positions in the sentence.

It is usually placed before the word(s) it refers to:
- **Anche** in Italia c'è bisogno di operai specializzati come in Germania.
  (In Italy there is a demand for specialized workers, as is the case in Germany.)
- Mia sorella si diverte ad andare in bicicletta e **anche** a suo marito piace molto.
  (My sister enjoys cycling and her husband really likes it, too.)

NEANCHE *(neither, not... either)*

It is used in negative sentence. It can occupy different positions in the sentence.
It is usually placed before the word(s) it refers to:
- Non so più arrivare a casa di mia zia e non ricordo **neanche** il nome del paese dove vive.
  (I don't know how to get to my aunt's home anymore and I can't remember the name of the village where she lives either.)

Anche and **neanche** add something to what has already been said.
When **neanche** is placed before the verb the negation **non** is not used.
- **Neanche** quel passante **sa** come arrivare in centro.
  (That passer-by doesn't know how to get to the centre either.)

DUNQUE *(so)*

It is used to introduce the consequence of what was previously said:
- Sono stanco, **dunque** mi prendo una settimana di ferie.
  (I'm tired, so I'll have a week's holiday.)
  (Due to the fact I am tired I have decided to take a week's holiday.)

CIOÈ   *(that is)*

It introduces the explanation of what was previously said:

– Non mi piace comprare molti vestiti, **cioè** mi compro solo i vestiti di cui ho realmente bisogno.
(I don't like buying a lot of clothes, that is/I mean I only buy the clothes I really need.)

SIA... SIA   *(both... and)*

They are used in *affirmative* sentences to join two parts of the sentence, more or less like **e**.
In modern Italian **sia... che** is often used:
– **Sia** Franco **sia (che)** Antonio giocano a calcio.
(Both Franco and Antonio play football.)

NÉ... NÉ   *(neither... nor)*

They are used in *negative* sentences to join two parts of the sentence:
– Non ho visto **né** Paolo **né** sua moglie al cinema.
(I didn't see Paolo nor his wife at the cinema.)

They could be replaced by **e neanche**:
– Non ho visto Paolo **e neanche** sua moglie al cinema.
(I didn't see Paolo nor his wife at the cinema.)

When **né... né** are placed before the verb the negation non is not used.
– **Né** Paolo **né** Luca parlano spagnolo.
(Neither Paolo nor Luca speaks Spanish)

93

coordinate conjunctions (2)
(tuttavia, perciò, ecc.) (nevertheless, therefore, etc.)

OPPURE, ALTRIMENTI *(or otherwise)*

They are used as synonyms of **o**:
- Regalale un libro **oppure** un cd. *(Give her a book or a CD.)*
- Prestami qualcosa da leggere, **altrimenti** dammi un video.
  (Lend me something to read, or give me a video, instead.)

PERÒ, TUTTAVIA *(but, however)*

They are used as synonyms of **ma**. **Tuttavia** is more formal and is preferably used in written Italian:
- Credo che la capitale del Burundi sia Bujumbura, **però** non ne sono sicuro.
  (I think Bujumbura is the capital of Burundi, but I'm not sure.)
- In Italia sono aumentate le esportazioni, **tuttavia** il mercato interno non si è ancora ripreso.
  (Italy has increased exports, however the home market still hasn't recovered.)

PURE *(also, too)*

It is used instead of **anche**, especially in the South of Italy:
- Recentemente sono stato a Sorrento e **pure** a Napoli.
  (I've been to Sorrento recently, and also Naples.)

NEPPURE, NEMMENO *(neither)*

They are synonyms of **neanche**:
- La strada statale per Cagliari è interrotta per il maltempo e **nemmeno** la provinciale è percorribile.
  (The main road to Cagliari is blocked due to the bad weather and the secondary road can't be used, either.)

Quando **neppure** e **nemmeno** sono prima del verbo non si mette la negazione **non**:

– Ho chiamato Sergio, ma non c'era e **neppure** sua sorella era in casa.

(I called Sergio, but he wasn't in and neither was his sister.)

PERCIÒ, QUINDI   (therefore, so)

They are used as synonyms of **dunque**:

– Suo padre è inglese, **perciò** anche lei ha il passaporto di quel paese.

(Her father is English, therefore she has a British passport, too.)

– Occorre aumentare la produzione, **quindi** bisogna chiedere agli operai di lavorare al sabato.

(Production needs to be increased, so we'll have to ask the workers to work on Saturdays, as well.)

94

subordinate conjunctions (1)
(poiché, quando, ecc.) (as, when, etc.)

■ **Subordinate conjunctions** are used to join two main clauses in a single sentence.

The result is a main clause and a subordinate clause, which is introduced by the subordinate conjunction.

Some conjunctions are followed by the indicative form, others by the subjunctive, others by the infinitive.

For conjunctions followed by the subjunctive, see Unità 70.

■ **Conjunctions of cause**

They introduce the *reason* behind what is stated in the main clause.

The verb is in the **indicative.**

PERCHÉ   *(because)*

– Fabrizia è preoccupata **perché** non ha abbastanza tempo per finire la sua ricerca.

(Fabrizia is worried because she hasn't got enough time to finish her reserarch.)

POICHÉ   *(as)*

– Non è possibile determinare con esattezza il numero degli stranieri in Italia, **poiché** molti sono immigrati illegalmente.

(It is impossible to ascertain the exact number of foreigners in Italy as many of then are illegal immigrants.)

DATO CHE/VISTO CHE/DAL MOMENTO CHE   *(since, as)*

– **Dato che/visto che/dal momento che** i membri dell'associazione sono tutti uomini, Lia non ha potuto aderirvi.

(Lia couldn't join the association, since all the members were men.)

SICCOME   *(since, as, because)*

– **Siccome** la vita in Italia è molto cara, molte famiglie devono fare attenzione a come spendono i soldi.
(Because life in Italy is so expensive, many families have to be careful how they spend their money.)

■ **Congiunzioni temporali**
The verb is in the **indicative**.

QUANDO   *(when)*

– **Quando** si vive in un paese straniero bisogna cercare di capire le abitudini di vita degli abitanti.
(When you live in a foreign country, you must try and understand the inhabitant's way of life.)

MENTRE   *(while)*

– **Mentre** mangio, mi piace ascoltare musica.
(I like listening to music while I eat.)

(NON) APPENA   *(as soon as)*

– **Non appena** arriverò a casa mi farò una doccia.
(As soon as I get home, I'll have a shower.)
The phrases *appena* and *non appena* are synonyms.

► **Non appena** does not have a negative meaning.

DA QUANDO   *(since)*

– **Da quando** vivo a Roma, esco tutte le sere.
(I have been out every evening since I came to live in Rome.)

Da quando introduces an action which began in the past and continues into the present. Note: the verb is in the *present*! Otherwise it can introduce an action which began in an earlier past and continued up to a more recent past:

– **Da quando** era cominciato a nevicare non si poteva uscire
di casa.
*(We weren't able to get out of the house from the moment
it started to snow.)*

FINCHÉ/FINO A QUANDO   *(up to when)*

– **Finché** avrà soldi Juan girerà l'Europa.
(Juan will travel around Europe until his money runs out.)

DOPO CHE   *(when, after)*

– **Dopo che** sarà passato il temporale, forse potremo andare
in piscina.
*(When the thunderstorm is over, we might be able to go to
the swimming pool.)*

PRIMA CHE   *(before)*

▶ The verbs is in the *subjunctive*.
See Unità 70 and Unità 89.

With many subordinate conjunctions the sentence can begin
either with the main clause or the subordinate clause:
– **Non appena** arriverò a casa mi farò una doccia.
Oppure: – Mi farò una doccia **non appena** arriverò a
casa.
*(As soon as I get home, I'm going to have a
shower.)*

subordinate conjunctions (2)

(anche se, se, ecc.) (even if, if etc.)

95

Conjunctions of purpose

They introduce the clause that expresses the *purpose*, the *aim* of the action in the main clause.

AFFINCHÉ *(so that)*

– **Affinché** voi possiate superare l'esame, vi indico alcuni testi fondamentali.
(I'll suggest some basic texts so that you can pass the exam.)

It is followed by the **subjunctive**. See Unità 70.

Conjunctions of result

They introduce the *result* of what is stated in the main clause.

COSÌ... CHE/COSICCHÉ *(so that)*

– Ieri sera ho lavorato fino a tardi **cosicché** oggi possiamo andare al mare.
(I worked until late yesterday evening so that we could go to the seaside today.)
– Ho preparato un risotto **così** salato **che** nessuno è riuscito a mangiarlo.
(The risotto I prepared was so salty that nobody could eat it.)

They are normally used with the indicative.

Conjunctions of concession/contrast

Anche se, benché, malgrado, nonostante, sebbene *(even though, although)*

ANCHE SE

It is the only conjunction of concession followed by the **indicative**. All the others are followed by the **subjunctive**:
– Anche se la casa nuova era pronta, la famiglia Pacini preferì rimanere ancora nel vecchio appartamento.

(Even though the new house was ready, the Pacini family preferred to stay in the old flat.)

BENCHÉ, MALGRADO, NONOSTANTE, SEBBENE

are synonyms and are all used in the same way; they are followed by the **subjunctive**. See Unità 70.

– **Malgrado** faccia brutto, ho voglia di uscire in bicicletta.
(Although the weather is bad, I still feel like going for a bike ride.)

Congiunzioni condizionali
They introduce the condition which is required by what is stated in the main clause.

SE *(if)*

See Unità 74: the hypothetical clause.

– Se tu non sei d'accordo non ci possiamo sposare.
(If you don't agree we can't get married.)

PURCHÉ, A PATTO CHE, A CONDIZIONE CHE

(as long as, provided) are synonyms and are all used in the same way; the are followed by the **subjunctive**. See Unità 70.

– **A condizione che** tu me li restituisca presto, ti presterò i soldi che ti occorrono.
(As long as you give it back to me soon, I'll lend you the money you need.)

Conjunctions of similarity/comparison
They express the way the action in the main clause happens.

COME SE *(as if)*

It is followed by the **subjunctive**:
– Mi parlò di sé **come se** fossimo amici da molti anni.
(He told me all about himself as if we had been friends for years.)

■ Conjunctions of exception and exclusion

They limit or exclude what is stated in the main clause.

SALVO CHE/TRANNE CHE *(except)*

They are followed by the **infinitive**.

– In casa Piero fa ogni cosa **tranne che** stirare.
(Piero does everything in the house except the ironing.)

A MENO CHE NON, SENZA CHE *(unless, without)*

They are followed by the subjunctive. See Unità 70.

– **A meno che non** si torni molto presto, non potrò venire a teatro con voi.
(Unless we get back home very early, I won't be able to come to the theatre with you.)

96

modifying nouns and adjectives
(bellino, casetta, ecc.) (pretty, little house, etc.)

Study the pictures.

*Guarda che bei **gattini**!*

The suffix - **ino/a** modifies the meaning of the noun.
These nouns are called **diminutivi**:
un gattino = un gatto piccolo
(a little cat)
una casina = una casa piccola
(a little house)

*Guarda che **gattone**!*

The suffix - **one/a** modifies the meaning of the noun.
These nouns are called **accrescitivi**:
un gattone = un gatto grande
(a big cat)
una casona = una casa grande
(a big house)

*- Guarda che **gattaccio**!*

The suffix - **accio/a** modifies the meaning of the noun.
These nouns are called **peggiorativi**:
un gattaccio = un gatto brutto e cattivo
(a horrible nasty cat)
un ragazzaggio = un ragazzo cattivo
(a bad boy)
una serataccia = una brutta serata
(a bad evening)

■ Study the examples.
un bambino bellino = un bambino piuttosto bello
(a pretty child)

ho dormito benino = ho dormito piuttosto bene
(I slept quite well)

■ Nouns, as well as adjectives and adverbs, can be modified in many other ways, by using different suffixes.
Sometimes it is not easy to understand whether it is a "diminutivo" or an ordinary noun.

Some other examples.

un quadr**etto** = un quadro piccolo *(a small picture)*
una finestr**ella** = una finestra piccola *(a small window)*
un ors**acchiotto** = un piccolo orso *(a little bear)*
un passer**otto** = un passero piccolo *(a little sparrow)*

All these suffixes may have an endearing nuance, i.e. express fondness or affection.

Other diminutivi have a pejorative or derogatory nuance instead, i.e. they express something negative.

un vesti**tuccio** *(a flimsy dress)*

In the following example, howerer, the suffix **-uccio** has an endearing rather than derogatory meaning.

È una **casuccia** molto accogliente. *(It's a very cosy little house.)*

■ Some nouns look like diminutivi, accrescitivi, etc., but they are not:

il postino   il lavandino   il maglione
(the postman   the sink   the pullover)

■ Verbs can have modified forms too: *ridacchiare, giocherellare, saltellare, (giggle, play about, skip)* etc.

Italian phonetic symbols

Vowels

/a/	/'mano/	mano
/e/	/'meta/	meta
/ɛ/	/'bɛllo/ /'bɛne/	bello bene
/i/	/i'dea/	idea
/o/	/'kome/	come
/ɔ/	/'ɔka/	oca
/u/	/'uno/	uno
/j/	/'piatto/ /'pjeno/	piatto pieno
/w/	/'kwadro/	quadro

Consonants

/p/	/'krepa/	crepa
/b/	/'banka/	banca
/t/	/'treno/	treno
/d/	/ka'dere/	cadere
/k/	/'parko/	parco
/g/	/'gatto/	gatto
/tʃ/	/'mantʃa/	mancia
/dʒ/	/'adʒitare/	agitare
/f/	/'fresko/	fresco
/v/	/'vino/	vino
/s/	/'sɛmpre/	sempre
/z/	/fanta'zja/	fantasia
/ʃ/	/ʃ'arpa/	sciarpa
/ts/	/por'tsjone/	porzione
/dz/	/dzaba'jone/	zabaione
/l/	/'fatʃile/	facile
/ʎ/	/'darʎi/	dargli
/r/	/'radjo/	radio
/m/	/'mjo/	mio
/n/	/'sano/	sano
/ɲ/	/'ɲɔkko/	gnocco

*The brackets contain the letter or word written in phonetic transcript.
The apostrophe is placed before the main stressed syllable of the
word, i.e. the stress is on the syllable after the apostrophe.*

Italian vowels and consonants

Italian vowels

```
                              /i/
                      /e/
              /ɛ/
      /a/
          /ɔ/
              /o/
                  /u/
```

There are seven vowel sounds in Italian. Many words contain diphthongs (two vowels together: quadro/'kwadro/, viene /'vjɛne/) and there are also some with triphthongs (three vowels together: miei /'miɛi/).

▶ In Italian the accent is not placed on the stressed syllable, except for when the stress is on the last vowel (e.g. virtù, realtà, più, già) and when it is necessary to distinguish between a few one syllable homonyms, for example:

da (preposition)	dà (verb *dare*)
li (pronoun)	lì (place adverb = là)
e (conjunction)	è (verb *essere*)

This feature of the Italian language can at times not only give rise to wrong pronunciation but can also cause misunderstanding, as some words have the same spelling but are pronounced differently in order to change meaning, for example:

principi ['printʃipi] (plural of principe/*princes*)
principi [prin'tʃipi] (plural of principio/*principles*)

Italian consonants

Double consonants

In Italian a word can have a double consonant.
The double consonants can be placed:

between two vowels	fatto	/'fatto/
between a vowel and an **r** an **l**	attraente	/attra'ɛnte/
	acclamare	/akkla'mare/

Here is a list of some words with double consonants.

p	cappello	/kap'pɛllo/
b	abbattere	/kap'pɛllo/
t	gatto	/'gatto/
d	caddi	/'kaddi/
k	tacco	/'takko/
g	leggo	/'leggo/
tʃ	accendere	/at'tʃendere/
dʒ	legge	/'leddʒe/
f	affitto	/af'fitto/
v	avventura	/avven'tura/
s	assieme	/as'sjɛme/
ts	razza	/'rattsa/
dz	razzo	/'raddzo/
m	mamma	/'mamma/
n	canna	/'kanna/
l	bello	/'bɛllo/
r	carro	/'karro/

The sound /z/ cannot be doubled.

The following letters are always pronounced as if double consonants when placed between two vowels:

ɲ	ragno	/'raɲɲo/
ʎ	figlio	/'fiʎʎo/
ʃ	fascia	/'faʃʃa/

▶ In the North of Italy there is a tendency to give less emphasis to the double consonants when speaking, whereas in Southern Italy single consonants tend to be doubled when positioned between two vowels.

▶ Students need to pay special attention to the pronunciation of double consonants. Sometimes if the double consonant is not pronounced, then the word can take on a different meaning.

penna	/'penna/	pena	/'pena/
sette	/'sɛtte/	sete	/'sete/
rette	/'rɛtte/	ete	/'rete/
fatto	/'fatto/	fato	/'fato/
sanno	/'sanno/	sano	/'sano/

Rules for written Italian

/ka/	**ca**sa	/'kasa/	/ga/	**ga**tto	/'gatto/
/ko/	**co**sta	/'kosta/	/go/	**go**la	/'gola/
/ku/	**cu**cina	/ku'tʃina/	/gu/	an**gu**stia	/an'gustia/
/ki/	**chi**amare	/kja'mare/	/gi/	a**ghi**	/'agi/
/ke/	ban**che**	/'banke/	/ge/	pa**ghe**	/'page/
/tʃa/	man**cia**	/'mantʃa/	/dʒa/	fa**gia**no	/fa'dʒano/
/tʃo/	mi**cio**	/'mitʃo/	/dʒo/	**gio**co	/'dʒɔko/
/tʃu/	**ciu**rma	/'tʃurma/	/dʒu/	**giu**sto	/'dʒusto/
/tʃe/	a**ce**to	/a'tʃeto/	/dʒe/	**ge**nte	/'dʒɛnte/
/tʃi/	cu**ci**re	/ku'tʃire/	/dʒi/	**gi**glio	/'dʒiʎʎo/

/ʃ/	**sci**mmia	/'ʃimmja/
	a**sci**ugare	/aʃʃu'gare/
/sk/	**sche**rzo	/'skertso/
	scala	/'skala/

| /kw/ | ac**qua** | /'akkwa/ | /gw/ | **gu**erra | /'gwɛrra/ |

| /ɲ/ | i**gn**orante | /'iɲɲorante/ |

| /ʎ/ | fi**gli**a | /'fiʎʎa/ |

| /ts/ | **z**io | /'tsio/ |

| /dz/ | **z**abaione | /dzaba'jone/ |

Glossary

abbreviation = it is usually a word which has been shortened, abbreviated, often for a particular use.

abstract nouns = they are nouns indicating qualities which cannot be not perceived by the senses. E.g.: amicizia (*friendship*), libertà (*freedom*), etc.

accrescitivi = they are modified nouns or adjectives (*cf. alteration*) which express the idea of something bigger, e.g.: una casona (*a big house*).

action = it is expressed by a verb.

active = it is a form of the verb. The subject performs the action, e.g.: il cane ha morso il bimbo (*the dog bit the little boy*), wheras in the passive form instead the subject undergoes the action, e.g.: il bimbo è stato morso dal cane (*The little boy was bitten by the dog.*).

adjective = bello, alto, mio, etc. They are words which are added to the noun (*cf.*) to describe it.

adverbs = they *are invariable words* (*cf.*) which are used to modify and specify the meaning of a verb or an adjective. Example: *parlare lentamente (speak slowly). Un libro molto bello (a very good book).*

adverbs of frequency = sempre, spesso, a volte, mai, etc. *(always, often, sometimes, never, etc.)*

affirmation = opposite of negation. *Cf. affirmative form.*

affirmative = positive. Affirmative form (*cf.*): for example in answers the affirmative form corresponds to "yes". It is the opposite of negative form (*cf.*).

affirmative form = a sentence in the affirmative form expresses a statement *(yes)*, it is the opposite of the negative form and it is different from the interrogative and interrogative-negative form.

affirmative sentence = *cf. affirmative form.*

agent = it is the sentence which indicates who/what performs the action in the passive. e.g.: la gazzella è stata uccisa dal leone (*The gazelle was killed by the lion.; The lion in the agent.*)

agreement = it is the sequence of the different parts of speech. For example article + noun *(cf.)* + adjective *(cf.)* are all in sequence according to the gender *(cf.)* and number *(cf.)*: le belle ragazze *(the pretty girls).*

alteration = alteration of the noun *(cf.)* or adjective *(cf.)*: it is a change in the form of the adjective or noun to express a different idea from the original one. For example: un ragazzo piccolo = un ragazzino *(a young boy).*

answer = what is said, done or written following a question.

auxiliary = auxiliary verbs are used to form compound tenses and the *passive (cf.).*

auxiliary verb = *avere (to have)* and *essere (to be),* in compound tenses. *Venire* and *andare* in the passive *(cf.).*

cardinal numbers = one, two, three, etc.

clause = a basic unit which expresses a thought. Two or more clauses joined together form a sentence.

combined form of the preposition with the article = di, a, da, in, con, su, per, tra, fra plus the definite article; e.g.: del, al, dal, etc. *(of the, to the, from the, etc.)*

combined personal pronoun = double personal pronouns: glielo, te le, etc. *(it to him, them to you, etc.)*

comparatives = adjectives or adverbs which express a comparison *(cf.)* between two or more elements.

comparativo di maggioranza = it is expressed by *più* followed by an adjective or an adverb. Example: Flavio *è più vecchio* di me *(Fabio is older than me.).* The comparison is in favour of the first element.

comparativo di minoranza = it is expressed by *meno* followed by an adjective or an adverb. Example: Flavio balla *meno elegantemente* di sua moglie *(Fabio doesn't dance as elegantly as his wife).* The comparison is in favour of the second element.

comparativo di uguaglianza = it is expressed by *tanto/quanto* or *così/come* with an adjective or an adverb. Example: Flavio è *(tanto) simpatico quanto* te *(Flavio is as nice as you.).* The comparison is in favour of neither of the two elements.

comparison = it can be between adjectives or adverbs, but also between nouns, pronouns and verbs.

comparison of adverbs = adverbs can also have comparative forms, example: Sara ora si comporta più intelligentemente di prima *(Sara behaves more intelligently now than she used to.).*

compound tenses = tenses formed by an auxiliary *(cf.)* and a main verb; e.g.: passato prossimo.

concrete nouns = they are nouns which indicate tangible things. E.g.: cane *(dog)*, libro *(book)*, uomo *(man)*, etc.

conditional = finite form *(cf.)* of the verb.

conditional = io avrei *(I would have).*

conjunction of cause = it introduces the *cause.* Poiché, dato che, etc. *(because, as)*

conjunction of concession = it introduces a clause of concession. It indicates a circumstance which takes place but does not modify what is stated in the main clause *(cf.)*. E.g.: *nonostante* faccia freddo, oggi pomeriggio esco in bicicletta *(I'm going to ride my bike this afternoon even though it's cold.).*

conjunction of condition = it introduces the *condition* which is required by what is stated in the main clause. E.g.: se domani farà bello, andrò al mare *(If the weather is nice tomorrow, I'll go to the seaside).*

conjunction of purpose = it introduces the clause which expresses the purpose of the action in the main clause. E.g.: Ti do 10 euro *affinché* tu vada al cinema *(I'm giving you 10 euro so you can go to the cinema).*

conjunction of result = it introduces the *consequence* of what is stated in the main clause. E.g.: ieri faceva brutto *cosicché* non sono andato al mare *(The weather wasn't good yesterday so I didn't go to the seaside).*

conjunction of time = it joins two clauses by taking time into consideration. E.g.: *quando, dopo che, mentre, etc. (when, after, while, etc.).* Es.: quando dormo non desidero essere disturbato *(I don't like being disturbed when I'm sleeping).*

consonant = in general, all the letters of the alphabet, except a, e, i, o, u.

coordinate conjunctions = they are used to join two main clauses. E.g.: *e, o, anche*, etc. (*and, or, also*, etc.) E.g.: c'è il sole e fa caldo *(The sun is shining and it's hot).*

definite article = il, lo, l', la, i, gli, le *(the).* Example: il cane *(the dog).*

demonstrative adjectives and pronouns = questo, quello, etc. *(this, that,* etc.)

demonstratives = demonstrative adjectives and pronouns; questo, quello, etc. They are used to indicate position in space and time.

diminutivi = they are modified adjectives or nouns *(cf. alteration)* which contain the idea of smallness and often express affection. E.g.: una ragazzina *(a young girl);* un giochino *(a little toy).*

diphthong = cf. *syllable.*

direct object = it answers the question: chi, che cosa? *(who, what?)* It undergoes the action of the subject. It has no preposition. E.g.: ho visto Luca *(I saw Luca).*

direct speech = when the exact words of a person are repeated without changing anything.
It is introduced by " ".

E.g.: *Spero che tu stia bene (I hope you are well),* but *speravo che tu stessi bene (I hoped you were well).*

ending = it is the variable part at the end of a noun, an adjective, a pronoun or a verb.

exception = something which does not follow the rule.

exclamations = words which are used to say something because of joy, admiration, etc. E.g.: *Che* bello! *(How nice!)*

expressions of place = words which define the place; they answer the question: dove? Da dove? etc. *(where, where from?,* etc.) There are different expressions of place: direction (it indicates movement), state (it does not indicate movement), origin, etc. E.g.: vivo *a Perugia,* ma vado spesso *a Roma* per lavoro. *(I live in Perugia, but I often go to Rome for work.)*

expressions of time = words which define time; they answer the question: quando? Per quanto tempo? Da quanto tempo? *(When? For how long? How long?)* They express the time, duration, etc. E.g.: *Lunedì sono stato a* *teatro per cinque ore (I spent five hours in the theatre on Monday.)*

feminine = grammatical gender, opposite to masculine. There are only two grammatical genders in Italian: feminine and masculine.

finite forms = forms of the verb which express the person. Indicative, conditional, subjunctive, imperative. E.g.: io vado (*I'm going*).

first person = singular: io (*I*), plural: noi (*we*).

formal = cf. formal *register*.

formal register = it refers to a way of using the language based on social context which usually expresses respect, it is typical of relationships between people who are neither friends nor relatives.
In the formal register the structure with Lei is used. It is the opposite of informal.

frequency = this indicates how many times a certain word or something else is used.

function = some functions: introducing oneself, greetings, etc.

future = io avrò (*I'll have*).

future in the past = it indicates an action which happens in a future time in relation to the past, however still past in relation to the present. E.g.: mi disse che sarebbe tornato presto (*He told me he would come back soon*).

future indicative = avrò (*I will have*).

future perfect = io avrò avuto (*I will have had*).

future perfect indicative = avrò avuto (*I will have had*).

future time = future/tomorrow, present/today, past/yesterday.

gender = it is the grammatical differentiation based on sex: feminine or masculine. It is important for the endings (*cf.*) of adjectives and nouns.

gerund = avendo (*having*).

gerund = indefinite form (*cf.*) of the verb.

hypothetical sentence = two or more clauses in which the subordinate (*cf.*) is introduced by se (*if*).

imperative = finite form (cf.) of the verb.

imperative with pronouns = compound form of the imperative with pronouns. E.g.: dagli (*give him*), parlategliene (*speak to him about it*).

imperfect = io avevo (*I had, I used to have*).

imperfect indicative = avevo (*I had, I used to have*).

imperfect subjunctive = che io avessi.

impersonal form = when the subject is not defined. Impersonal subjects are: *si* and, in some cases, *tu*, *loro*, etc.

impersonal verb = a verb without a definite subject.

indefinite article = un, uno, una, un' (*a/an*). Example: *un cane (a dog)*.

indefinite forms = forms of the verb which do not express the person. Gerund, infinitive, participle. E.g.: andando (*going*).

indefinite pronouns or adjectives = pronouns or adjectives which give indefinite information. E.g.: qualche (*some, any*), qualcosa (*something, anything*), etc.

indirect object = in general, any phrase containing a preposition.

infinitive = indefinite form (*cf.*) of the verb.

informal = cf. *informal register*.

informal register = it refers to a way of using the language based on social context which usually expresses friendship and friendliness, it is typical of relationships between people who are either friends or relatives. In the informal register the structure with tu is used. It is the opposite of formal.

interrogative form = a sentence in the interrogative form expresses a question, it is different from the negative and affirmative forms.

interrogative-negative form = a sentence in the interrogative-negative form expresses a negative question, it is different from the negative and affirmative forms.

intonation = they way the voice rises or falls when pronouncing a word or sentence.

intransitive verb = a verb which is not followed by the direct object (*cf.*). It does not answer the question: chi/che cosa? (*Who/what?*) E.g.: io parlo con mia madre (*I'm speaking to my mother*).

invariable = it does not change.

irregular forms = when they do not follow the rule.

letter = any element of the alphabet: a, b, c, etc.

main clause = clause which governs other clauses.

masculine = grammatical gender, different from the feminine. There are two grammatical genders in Italian: feminine and masculine.

modified forms = the modified forms of nouns, adjectives or adverbs are diminutivi, accrescitivi, etc. *(cf.)*.

monosyllables = words containing only one syllable *(cf.)*.

negative form = a sentence in the negative form expresses a negation (*no*), it is the opposite of the affirmative form and different from the interrogative and interrogative-negative forms.

negative sentence = cf. *negative form*.

non = word used to deny, say no.

noun = words which indicate animals, people, things, etc.

number = it is the way to differentiate grammatically between singular and plural *(cf.)*. It is important for the endings *(cf.)* of verbs, adjectives and nouns.

object = *(cf.)* direct object; indirect object.

object personal pronoun = personal pronouns which act as the object: mi, ti, ci, me, te, etc. *(me, you, us, etc.)*

opposite = antonym.

order = command.

ordinal numbers = first, second, third, etc.

participle = indefinite form *(cf.)* of the verb.

partitive = it expresses a part

of a whole. *Partitive ne*, e.g.: "Quanto zucchero vuoi?" "Ne prendo due cucchiaini." (How much sugar do you take? I'll have two teaspoonfuls.)

passato prossimo = tense of the indicative. Io ho avuto *(I had, I have had)*.

passato remoto = tense of the indicative. Io ebbi *(I had)*.

passive = it is a form of the verb. The subject undergoes the action; e.g.: il bimbo è stato morso dal cane *(The little boy was bitten by the dog.)*. In the active form instead the subject performs the action; e.g.: il cane ha morso il bimbo *(The dog bit the little boy)*.

past and past perfect subjunctive = che io abbia avuto, che io avessi avuto.

past gerund = avendo avuto *(having had)*.

past participle = avuto.

past perfect = avevo avuto *(I had had)*.

past perfect indicative = avevo avuto *(I had had)*.

past time = past/yesterday, future/tomorrow, present/today.

peggiorativi = they are modified adjectives or nouns *(cf. alteration)* which contain a negative idea and express a negative opinion. E.g.: ragaz-zaccio *(a bad boy)*.

perfect conditional = io avrei avuto *(I would have had)*.

perfect infinitive = avere avuto *(to have had)*.

person = io, tu, lui/lei, noi, voi, loro *(I, you, he/she/it, we, you, they)*.

personal pronoun = pronoun which indicates person or thing.

phonetic symbol = a special way of writing words which reproduces the way they are pronounced: cane = /'kane/.

phrases = expressions or sen-tences; groups of two or more words which form a unit; e.g.: di solito, a proposito, andare giù *(usually, by the way, go down)*.

plural = it indicates the number of people or things above one.

polite form = when you address someone in a formal way, using the structure with Lei.

possessive adjectives and pronouns = mio, tuo, suo, etc.

prefix = particle added to the beginning of a word.

preposition = di, a, da, in, con, su, per, tra, fra *(of, to, from, in, with, on, for, bet-ween/among)*.

present indicative = io ho *(I have)*.

present infinitive = avere *(to have)*.

present participle = avente.

present subjunctive = che io abbia.

present time = present/today, past/yesterday, future/tomorrow.

pronoun = word which repla-ces the noun.

reflexive verbs = verbs in which the action falls back onto the subject; e.g.: io mi lavo *(I'm getting washed)*.

regular forms = when they follow the rule.

relative pronoun = it refers back to a previous noun or sentence. Che, cui, il quale, etc. *(who, which, that, etc.)*

reported speech = when what was said by someone is reported changing some ele-ments.

It is often introduced by the verb *dire* (say, tell) and che *(that)*. E.g.: Giovanni mi *ha detto che* domani...
(Giovanni told me that tomor-row ...)

rule = the dominant norm in a language.

second person = singular: tu *(you)*, plural: voi *(you)*.

sentence = two or more clauses joined together, forming a meaningful unit.

sequence of tenses = it is the agreement of the tenses, for example between main clause and subordinate clause (*cf.*).

singular = it indicates a number of people or things equivalent to one.

spregiativi = they are modified adjectives or nouns (*cf. alteration*) which contain a negative idea and express scorn. E.g.: ragazzaccio (*a very bad boy*).

stem = part of the word which is left after the ending (*cf.*) has been taken away.

stress = it is a symbol (accent) or usually a certain intonation (*cf.*) of the voice which indicates the stressed vowel (*cf.*).

stressed forms of the personal pronouns = e.g.: *a me, a te, a noi*, etc. They are stressed because they are strong, they emphasise the pronoun.

stressed pronouns = the stressed forms of personal pronouns (*cf.*) are for example: *a me, a te, a noi*, etc.

stressed vowel = vowel where the stress falls.

structure = the way the elements of a language are organized; or, sometimes: grammatical or syntactical rule.

subject = the person, thing, etc. which performs the action.

subject personal pronoun = io, tu, lui/lei, noi, voi, loro. They act as subject (*cf.*).

subordinate clause = clause which depends on the main clause.

subordinate conjunction = it is used to join two clauses in a single sentence, one clause is the main clause, the other is the subordinate.

suffix = particle added at the end of a word.

superlatives = adjectives or adverbs which express a certain quality at its maximum.

superlativo assoluto = there is no comparison with other elements; it ends in -issimo. E.g.: un gatto bellissimo (*a very pretty cat*).

superlativo relativo = there is a comparison with other elements. E.g.: il più bel film di Fellini (*Fellini's best film*).

syllable = basic unit in a language, formed by a vowel or by a vowel preceded and followed by one or more consonants.

Sometimes there are two or more vowels together (diphthong, triphthong).

synonym = a word which means the same thing as another.

term = word.

third person = singular: lui/lei (*he/she*), plural: loro (*they*).

transitive verb = verb followed by an object *(cf.)*. It answers the question chi/che cosa? (*who/what?*) E.g.: mangio una mela (*I'm eating an apple*).

trapassato remoto = ebbi avuto *(I had had)*.

trapassato remoto indicative = ebbi avuto *(I had had)*.

unstressed forms of the personal pronouns = e.g.: *mi, ti, ci*, etc. They are unstressed because they are weak, they are supported by the verb.

unstressed pronouns = the unstressed forms of personal pronouns *(cf.)* are for example: *mi, ti, ci*, etc.

variable = something which changes. E.g.: masculine/feminine, singular/plural, etc.

verb = word which indicates an action or a way of being.

vezzeggiativi = they are modified adjectives and nouns *(cf. alteration)* which express affection. E.g.: la mia casetta *(my little house)*.

virtù [vir'tu] capitano [kapi'tano].

vowel = the letters: a, e, i, o, u.

word stress = it is the intonation of the voice which stresses a particular syllable *(cf.)*

Index

The numbers refer to the units, not the page.

A	24, 27, 29
a (for place)	24
a (for time)	27
A condizione che	70
A costo di	89
A forza di	89
A meno che non	70
A patto che	70
Abbastanza	22, 57
Accanto a	26
Accrescitivi	96
Adjectives	**10**
Adverbs	**21**
Affinché	70,96
Agreement of the past participle	31
Adverbs	**21**
of manner, time, place, quantity, doubt	21
of frequency	22
confirming and denying adverbs	21
Al	23
Alcuno	55
Altrimenti	**93**
Anche	92
Anche se	95
Anni	18,23,27
Appena, non appena	94
Articles	**5, 6**
Attraverso	26
Avere, infinitive, present indicative	2
Bello	10
Benché	10
Buono	10
Cardinal numbers	**15**
Che	19, 20
Che, relative pronouns	45
Che cosa	19
Che ore sono?	17
Chi	19, 45
Chiunque	56

217

Ci	42
Ciascuno	55
Cioè	92
Codesto	12
Combined preposition with the definite article	**23**
preposition of place	24
prepositions of time	27
Come	20
Come se	95
Comparatives	**59, 61, 62, 70**
irregular comparatives	61
comparativo di maggioranza	59
comparativo di minoranza	59
comparativo di uguaglianza	59
comparative forms of adverbs	62
Con	30
Conditional	**49, 50, 51, 74**
conditional	49, 50, 74
conditional - form	49
conditional - use	50, 74
perfect conditional	51, 74
Coordinate conjunctions	**92, 93**
Così... che/cosicché	95
Così... come	59
Cui	45
Da	**25, 28, 30**
da (for place)	25
da (for time)	28
da dove	20
da quando	94
da... a... (for time)	28
Dal momento che	94
Da & per + infinitive	87
Dates, 20 dicembre 1999	18, 27
Dato che	94
Davanti a	25
Definite articles	**5**
definite article with possessives	11
definite articles with prepositions	23
Indefinite article	6
Dei, degli, delle	6, 23
Del	23

Demonstratives — 12, 13
    demonstrative adjectives — 12
    demonstrative pronouns — 13
Dentro — 25
Di — 28, 29
    di (for time) — 28
Di chi — 19
Di fianco a — 26
Dietro — 25
Diminutivi — 96
Dopo — 28, 88
    dopo che — 94
    dopo che + future perfect — 47
    dopo che + trapassato remoto — 80
    dopo + perfect infinitive — 88
Dove — 20
Dunque — 92
Durante — 28
E — 92
Exclamations — 20
Essere, infinitive, present indicative — 1
Finché/fino a quando — 94
Fino a — 26, 28
    fino a (for place) — 26
    fino a (for time) — 28
Fra/tra — 25, 30
    Fra/tra (for place) — 25
Fuori — 25
Future — 37
Future perfect — 47
Gender of nouns — 7
Gerund — 90
Hypothetical clauses — 74
Il cui, etc. — 46
Il più..., superlativo relativo — 60
Il, lo, la, i, gli, le — 5
Il/la quale, i/le quali — 46
Imperative — 63, 64, 65
    Imperative - form — 63
    Imperative with pronouns — 64
    Imperative - use — 65

Index

Imperfect   **33, 34, 36, 52, 74**
     Imperfect - form   33
     Imperfect - use   34, 36, 52, 74
Impersonal si   **78**
Impersonal form   **79**
In   24, 27, 30
     In (for place)   24
     In (for time)   27
In modo da   89
Indefiniti   **54, 55, 56, 57, 58**
Indefinite - adjectives and pronouns   55
Indefinite - adjectives   54
Indefinite - pronouns   56
Indefinite forms   **84, 85, 86, 88, 89**
Infinitive   **84, 85, 86, 87, 88, 89**
     present infinitive   84, 85, 86, 88, 89
     perfect infinitive   88
     infinitive with other expressions   89
Invece di   89
Io, tu, lui, etc.   38
Irregular plurals of nouns   9
Lo, la, li, le, pronouns   **40**
Lontano da   26
Loro, impersonal form   79
Lungo   26
Ma   92
Mai   22
Malgrado   70
Masculine and feminine nouns   **7**
Me, te, stressed personal pronouns   39
Me lo, te lo, glielo, combined personal pronouns   44
Meglio, comparative form of the adverb   62
Meno   59, 60
Mentre   28, 94
Mi, ti, unstressed personal pronouns   40
Mica   21
Migliore, irregular comparatives   61
Mio, tuo, suo, possessive adjectives and pronouns   61
Modifying the noun   **96**
Molto   22, 58
Ne   42
Ne partitivo   43

Né... né	91
Neanche	92
Negative, interrogative and interrogative-negative form	**1**
Nel	23
Nel caso che	70
Nemmeno	93
Neppure	93
Nessuno	55
Niente/nulla	56
Nonostante	70
O	92
Ogni	54
Ognuno	56
Oppure	93
Ordinal numbers	15, 16
Parecchio	57
Participle	**91**
past participle	31, 91
agreement of the past participle	31
present participle	91
Passato prossimo	**31, 32, 36**
Passato remoto	**35, 36**
Passive	**75, 76**
Passive structure with si	77
Past perfect	**48**
Peggio, comparative form of the adverb	62
Peggiorativi	96
Peggiore, irregular comparatives	61
Per	26, 27, 30
per (for place)	26
per for time)	27
Perché	20, 94
Perciò	93
Però	93
Personal pronouns	**38, 39, 40, 44**
Subject personal pronouns	38
Object personal pronouns - stressed forms	39
Object personal Pronouns - unstressed forms	40
Combined personal pronouns	44
Più	59, 60
Plural of nouns	**8, 9**
Poco	22, 57

Index

Poiché	94
Possessive adjectives	**11**
Possessive pronouns	**11**
Potrei	14
Prepositions	**23, 24, 27, 29, 30**
Present indicative	**3, 4**
present indicative (regular verbs)	3
present indicative (irregular verbs)	4
present indicative of the verb essere	1
present indicative of the verb avere	2
Prima	28
prima che	70, 89, 94
prima di	89
Primo, secondo, terzo, ordinal numbers	16
Proprio	11
Purché	70
Pure	93
Qualche	54
Qualcosa	56
Qualcuno	56
Quale	19
Qualsiasi/qualunque	54
Quando	20, 47, 94
Quanto	19, 20
Question words	**19, 20**
Questo, quello, demonstratives	12, 13
Quindi	93
Reflexive verbs	**41**
Relative pronouns	45, 46
Reported speech	**81, 82, 83**
Salvo che/tranne che	94
Se	74, 95
Sé	39
Sebbene	70
Secoli	18, 23, 27
Sequence of tenses	**71, 72, 73**
Sempre	22
Senza	89
Senza che	70
Sia... sia	92
Siccome	94
Sotto	25
Spesso	22

Stare + gerund 52
Stare per + infinitive 53
Su 30
Su (for place) 25
Subordinate conjunctions **94, 95**
Subjunctive 66, 67, 68, 69, 70
  imperfect subjunctive - form 67
  past and past perfect subjunctive - form 68
  present subjunctive - form 66
  subjunctive - use 69, 70
Sul 23
Superlatives **60, 61, 62**
  irregular superlatives 61
  superlative form of the adverb 62
  superlativo assoluto 60
  superlativo relativo 60
Tanto 58
Tanto... quanto 59
Tenses and forms of the verb:
  io sono, etc. 1
  io ho, etc. 2
  io ho, present indicative 2, 3, 4
  io ho avuto, passato prossimo 31, 32, 36
  io avevo, imperfect 34, 36, 52, 74
  io ebbi, passato remoto 35, 36
  io avrò, future 37
  io avrò avuto, past perfect 47
  io avevo avuto, past perfect 48
  io avrei, conditional 49, 50
  io avrei avuto, perfect conditional 51, 74
  abbi...!, affermative form of the imperative 63, 65
  (che) io abbia, present subjunctive 66, 69, 70
  (che) io abbia avuto, past subjunctive 66, 68, 69, 70
  (che) io avessi avuto, past perfect subjunctive 68, 69, 70
  (che) io avessi, imperfect subjunctive 67, 68, 69, 70
  io ebbi avuto, trapassato remoto 80
  io sto mangiando 52
  io sto per mangiare 53
  avendo, gerund 90
  avente, present participle 91
  avuto, past participle 31, 91
  avere, present infinitive 2, 84, 85, 86, 88, 89
  avere avuto, perfect infinitive 88

Index

The time	17
Tra/fra (for time)	27
Trapassato prossimo	**48**
Trapassato remoto	**80**
Troppo	22, 58
Tu, impersonal form	79
Tuttavia	93
Tutto	58
Un po'	22, 57
Un, uno, una, un'	6
Uno, due, tre, cardinal numbers, etc.	15
Uno, indefinite	56
Uno, impersonal form	79
Vari, diversi	57
Venire/andare, passive	76
Verbs/adjectives + a + infinitive	85
Verbs/adjectives + di + infinitive	86
Vicino a	26
Visto che	94
Vorrei	14

Diagnostic test

with answer key

Unità 1

1. Voi .... austriaci.
   a) siamo   b) sono   c) siete   d) è

2. Di dove................(tu)?
   a) sono   b) sei   c) è   d) siamo

Unità 2

3. Quanti anni (tu) .... ? .... 25 anni.
   a) hai, abbiamo   b) ho, hanno
   c) hai, ho   d) ho, hai

4. Fa caldo e (noi) ....
   a) avete sonno   b) hanno fame
   c) abbiamo sonno   d) abbiamo sete

Unità 3-4

5. Mio padre .... in banca.
   a) lavori   b) lavora
   c) lavore   d) lavoro

6. Al mattino (io) .... colazione al bar.
   a) fai   b) faccio
   c) fa   d) fate

7. Come (tu) .... ? Bene, grazie.
   a) sto   b) state
   c) stai   d) sta

Unità 5-6

8. ...... zio di Francesco è .... dottore dell'ospedale.
   a) il, un   b) la, uno
   c) lo, un   d) lo, uno

9. .... Parigi è .... capitale della Francia.
   a) X, il   b) la, la
   c) il, X   d) X, la

10. la scuol.....   ..... scuol.....
   a) scuolo, le scuoli   b) scuola, le scuole
   c) scuoli, gli scuole   d) scuole, la scuoli

11. il libr......   ..... libr.....
   a) libri, gli libri   b) libro, le libre
   c) libro, i libri   d) libra, i libri

12. la stazion.....   ..... stazion.....
   a) stazione, le stazioni   b) staziona, le stazione
   c) stazioni, i stazioni   d) staziono, i stazione

Unità 10

13. L'appartamento di Francesca ha le porte ....
   a) verdi   b) verde
   c) verda   d) verdo

14. Angelo è un .... amico
   a) buono   b) buona
   c) buon   d) buon'

Unità 11

15. Gianni telefona ogni mese ai .... amici in Francia.
   a) suo   b) suoi
   c) sue   d) sui

16. Quando vai a salutare .... madre?
   a) tuoi   b) tuo
   c) tue   d) tua

Unità 12-13

17. Di chi sono .... chiavi?
   a) queste   b) questi
   c) questo   d) questa

18. Qual è tuo figlio? .... là in fondo con la maglietta verde.
   a) questo   b) codesto
   c) quello   d) ciò

Unità 14

19. (Io) .... un piatto di spaghetti, per favore.
   a) vorrebbe
   b) potrei
   c) vorrei
   d) potrebbe

Unità 15-16

20. 3.456.000 = ...
   a) tre milioni quattrocentocinquantaseimila
   b) tre milioni quattrocentocinquantaseimille
   c) tremilioniquattrocentocinquantasei
   d) tre milioni quattrocentocinquantasei

21. 7/11 = ...
   a) settimi undicesimi
   b) sette undici
   c) settimo undici
   d) sette undicesimi

Unità 17

22. Che ore sono? Sono le (8.45) ....
   a) otto e un quarto
   b) nove e tre quarti
   c) nove e un quarto
   d) nove meno un quarto

Unità 18

23. Chiara è nata ....
   a) nel tre luglio mille novecento settantanove
   b) al tre luglio mille novecentosettantanove
   c) il tre luglio millenovecentosettantanove
   d) tre luglio millenovecento settantanove

Unità 19-20

24. .... fai domani sera? Esci con me?
   a) come
   b) dove
   c) che cosa
   d) chi

25. .... è il tuo numero di telefono?
   a) come
   b) quale
   c) qual
   d) che

Unità 21-22

26. Se vai a studiare in Francia, impari .... il francese
   a) facilemente
   b) facilemento
   c) facilmente
   d) facilmenta

27. Io vengo .... Inghilterra.
   a) dal
   b) dall'
   c) dalla
   d) dallo

28. In estate ci sono molti frutti .... alberi.
   a) sugli
   b) sui
   c) sulli
   d) su

Unità 24-25-26

29. Abito .... Napoli, ... Via Cuoco 32.
   a) in, in
   b) a, in
   c) a, a
   d) in, a

30. Domani andiamo .... ristorante "I Pifferi".
   a) dal
   b) in
   c) nel
   d) al

31. La penna è .... il libro.
   a) dentro
   b) fra
   c) lungo
   d) davanti

32. C'è un bar .... la macelleria e il tabaccaio.
   a) dentro
   b) lungo
   c) lontano
   d) tra

33. Dormo sempre .... divano del soggiorno.
   a) dentro
   b) sul
   c) dietro
   d) nel

Unità 27-28

34. Ci vediamo .... due ore.
   a) in
   b) a
   c) tra
   d) da

35. In Italia le scuole iniziano .... settembre.
   a) con
   b) al
   c) tra
   d) in

36. La farmacia è chiusa .... lunedì.
   a) fino a
   b) durante
   c) mentre
   d) a

Unità 29-30

37. In casa porto sempre una tuta .... ginnastica.
   a) di
   b) a
   c) da
   d) per

38. Vorrei un panino .... prosciutto e una lattina .... birra.
   a) di, di
   b) al, alla
   c) al, di
   d) con, alla

39. Mi piace, d'estate, andare in giro .... moto.
   a) con
   b) per
   c) con il
   d) in

Unità 31-32

40. Con chi .... al telefono ieri sera?
   a) parlando
   b) hai parlare
   c) hai parlato
   d) hai parluto

41. .... a Roma in treno.
   a) ho andato
   b) sono andare
   c) sono andato
   d) ho vadato

42 Non ho capito quello che ....
   a) hai detto
   b) hai diciuto
   c) hai ditto
   d) sei

Unità 33-34

43. Mi canti ancora quella canzone che mi ....tempo fa?
   a) cantavo
   b) cantavi
   c) cantevi
   d) cantevo

44. Mentre .... sulla pianta di mele sono caduto.
   a) sono salito
   b) salivo
   c) ho salito
   d) salendo

Unità 35

45. Quando .... suo figlio, Antonio si mise a ridere.
   a) vede
   b) vide
   c) ha visto
   d) ebbe visto

Unità 36

46. Mentre (io) .... a lavorare, (io) .... mio zio.
   a) andavo, incontratti
   b) andai, incontravo
   c) andavo, ho incontrato
   d) sono andato, incontrati

Unità 37

47. Clara e Cinzia .... per le vacanze in giugno.
   a) partiremo
   b) partaranno
   c) partiranno
   d) partireno

Unità 38

48. .... venite a cena da noi stasera.
   a) voi
   b) tu
   c) loro
   d) noi

Unità 39-40

49. Vado in centro. Vuoi venire con ....
   a) io
   b) mi
   c) me
   d) te

50. Ho parlato con Anna e .... ho detto tutto.
   a) gli
   b) la
   c) ci
   d) le

51. Dov'è tua sorella? Non .... dall'anno scorso.
   a) la ho più visto
   b) l'ho più vista
   c) l'ho più visto
   d) le ho più vista

Unità 41

52. Io .... i capelli ogni sera.
   a) mi lavo
   b) si lava
   c) mi lava
   d) si lavo

53. Ieri Giovanna .... alle 11.
   a) si ha alzata
   b) si è alzato
   c) si è alzata
   d) se ha alzata

Unità 42

54. Quando vai a Roma? .... vado sabato.
   a) si   b) ce
   c) ne   d) ci

55. Come fai a conoscere questa storia? Me .... ha parlato
   Carla.
   a) ci   b) ne
   c) la   d) lo

Unità 43

56. Questo vino è molto buono. ...... vuoi un bicchiere?
   a) ne   b) lo
   c) la   d) ci

Unità 44

57. Chi mi presta una penna? .... presto io.
   a) ce lo   b) te la
   c) ti la   d) te lo

58. Chi offre una sigaretta a Luigi? .... offro io.
   a) gliela   b) lui la
   c) gli la   d) la gli

Unità 45-46

59. Ti presento Thomas e Günther. Sono amici .... vengono
   da Bonn.
   a) cui   b) chi
   c) che   d) li quali

60. Ti piace la camicia .... ho comprato stamattina?
   a) chi   b) la quale
   c) cui   d) che

61. La Germania è una nazione .... vivrei volentieri.
   a) in la quale   b) nella cui
   c) in la cui   d) nella quale

Unità 47

62. Ti telefonerò dopo che .... a Torino.
   a) sarò arrivato
   b) sarei arrivato
   c) arriverò
   d) arriverei

Unità 48

63. .... di lavorare, quando Angelo disse che voleva aiutarmi.
   a) avevo già finito
   b) finivo
   c) già finivo
   d) ebbi finito

Unità 49-50

64. Signor Schianchi, ... mangiare meno grassi.
   a) dovrebbe
   b) doverebbe
   c) deverebbe
   d) devrebbe

Unità 51

65. ....alla festa, ma non avevo proprio tempo.
   a) verrei
   b) sarei venuto
   c) avrei venuto
   d) verrò

Unità 52

66. Ti .... già da un'ora. Perché sei sempre in ritardo?
   a) aspettando
   b) sto aspettando
   c) sto per aspettare
   d) sto per aspettando

Unità 53

67. Corri, corri, il treno ....
   a) stava partendo
   b) stava per partire
   c) sta per partendo
   d) sta per partire

Unità 54

68. Lavoro ancora .... giorno poi vado in ferie.
   a) alcuno
   b) ogni
   c) qualche
   d) alcuni

Unità 55

69. Sono stanco. Ho bisogno di .... settimane
di vacanza.

   a) qualche
   b) alcune
   c) alcuni
   d) ogni

Unità 56

70. Prendi il giornale e guarda se c'è .... di bello
al cinema.

   a) qualcosa
   b) qualcose
   c) uno
   d) qualcuno

Unità 57

71. C'è .... birra in frigo, o ne serve ancora per
la festa?

   a) poco
   b) un po'
   c) parecchio
   d) abbastanza

Unità 58

72. Non vedo più Franco da .... tempo. Non lo
riconoscerei più.

   a) tutto
   b) troppi
   c) tanto
   d) tanti

Unità 59

73. Francesco è più grasso .... Carlo.

   a) che
   b) quanto
   c) di
   d) del

74. Mi piace di più leggere .... scrivere.

   a) di
   b) che
   c) dello
   d) quanto

Unità 60

75. Questo film è molto lungo, anzi è ....

   a) lungissimo
   b) molto lunghissimo
   c) assai lungissimo
   d) lunghissimo

76. Poldo capisce tutto. È il cane .... intelligente ....
    io abbia mai avuto.
    a) più, di   b) meno, di
    c) meno, che   d) più, che

Unità 61

77. Sono veramente contento. All'esame ho ottenuto un
    .... risultato.
    a) ottimo   b) pessimo
    c) minimo   d) il maggiore

Unità 62

78. Mi sono comportato ...., ma non è
    servito a niente.
    a) in modo benissimo   b) nel modo benissimo
    c) nel modo migliore   d) nel modo meglio

Unità 63-64-65

79. (Tu) .... quest'acqua. Non vedi com'è
    sporca?
    a) non bevi   b) non bere
    c) non beva   d) non bevere

80. Signor Bruni, ... dal direttore, perché le vuole parlare.
    a). va'   b) vada
    c) vai   d) andi

81. Non posso andare a comprare il giornale. .... tu quando
    esci, per favore.
    a) me lo compra   b) comprimelo
    c) compracelo   d) compramelo

Unità 66-67-68-69-70

82. Credo che, per superare l'esame, tu .... studiare
    di più.
    a) deva   b) devi
    c) debba   d) debbi

83. Pensavo che .... necessario prendere i biglietti il
    giorno prima.
    a) fossi   b) era
    c) fosse   d) eri

84. .... fossi già stanco, ho continuato a correre
    fino a casa.
    a) sebbene   b) anche se
    c) a patto che   d) nel caso che

Unità 71

85. Sono sicuro che ieri Anna .... un nuovo lavoro.
    a) ha trovato   b) abbia trovato
    c) trova   d) avesse trovato

86. L'anno scorso ero sicuro che (noi) .... questa
    primavera.
    a) ci saremmo sposati   b) ci sposeremmo
    c) ci avremmo sposati   d) ci sposeremo

Unità 72-73

87. Dubito che tu .... le mie vere intenzioni.
    a) capisci   b) hai capito
    c) abbia capito   d) avrai capito

88. Clara vorrebbe che qualcuno l'............................ a
    spostare la libreria.
    a) aiuta   b) aiutava
    c) avrebbe aiutata   d) aiutasse

89. Avrei desiderato che l'estate scorsa noi...............................
    di più al mare.
    a) ci eravamo divertiti   b) ci divertiremmo
    c) ci avessimo divertiti   d) ci fossimo divertiti

Unità 74

90. Se mi .... 50 euro, te li .... domani.
    a) prestassi, restituirò   b) prestassi, avrei restituiti
    c) presti, restituirò   d) presti, restituirei

91. Se Laura .... in tempo di essere ammalata,
.... subito all'ospedale.
a) si sarebbe accorta, sarebbe andata
b) si fosse accorta, sarebbe andata
c) si avrebbe accorta, sarebbe andata
d) si accorgesse, sarebbe andata

Unità 75-76

92. Il debito pubblico dei paesi in via di sviluppo ....
cancellato.
a) va essere   b) deve essere
c) è andato   d) è dovuto

93. .... è stato scritto questo libro?
a) per chi   b) chi
c) di chi   d) da chi

Unità 77

94. In questo parco non .... accendere fuochi.
a) si possiamo   b) si possono
c) si hanno potuto   d) si hanno dovuto

Unità 78

95. D'estate, in montagna, ... bene, perché c'è
fresco.
a) uno si sta   b) ci si stanno
c) si stanno   d) si sta

Unità 79

96. .... si stanca a trascorrere tutto il giorno senza far
niente.
a) tu   b) uno
c) loro   d) si

Unità 80

97. Dopo che .... la partita di calcio, scoppiarono
gli incidenti.
a) fu finita   b) ebbe finita
c) finiva   d) aveva finita

98. Paolo dice: "Oggi torno a casa" Paolo dice
    che..................
    a) oggi torno a casa   b) quel giorno torna a casa
    c) domani torna a casa   d) oggi torna a casa

99. Paolo disse: "Oggi vado al ristorante".
    Paolo disse che ....
    a) ieri andava al ristorante
    b) oggi va al ristorante
    c) ieri è andato al ristorante
    d) quel giorno andava al ristorante

100. Paolo chiede a Pino: "Tuo fratello si chiama Andrea?"
     Paolo chiede a Pino se ....
     a) suo fratello si chiama Andrea
     b) tuo fratello si chiamasse Andrea
     c) suo fratello si chiami Andrea
     d) tuo fratello si chiami Andrea

Unità 84

101. Per arrivare in piazza Duomo è necessario....................
     a destra.
     a) di voltare   b) da voltare
     c) voltare   d) per voltare

Unità 85-86

102. Speriamo .... un'altra volta. Ci siamo
     divertiti con voi!
     a) a incontrarvi   b) incontrarvi
     c) che vi incontriamo   d) di incontrarvi

103. Filippo era convinto .... il migliore della classe.
     a) a essere   b) di essere
     c) che sia   d) essere

104. Non sono mai riuscito .... al lotto.
     a) di vincere   b) per vincere
     c) a vincere   d) che vinco

105. Claudio è abituato .... fino a tardi.
   a) a dormire   b). per dormire
   c). che dorma   d). di dormire

Unità 87

106. Volete qualcosa ....?
   a) da bere
   b) a bere
   c) per bere
   d) di bere

Unità 88

107. Dopo .... alla sua famiglia, Paolo
   ripartì per l'India.
   a) telefonato   b) essere telefonato
   c) aver telefonato   d) telefonare

108. L'architetto è stato premiato per ....
   uno splendido progetto.
   a) essere disegnato   b) disegnato
   c) disegnare   d) aver disegnato

Unità 89

109. .... uscire dobbiamo chiudere le finestre.
   a) prima che   b) prima
   c) prima di   d) prima da

110. È difficile superare questo test .... studiare la
   grammatica.
   a) senza di   b) senza
   c) senza da   d) senza che

Unità 90

111. .... troppo a cena, quella notte non sono
   riuscito a dormire.
   a) mangiando   b) mangiato
   c) avendo mangiato   d) poiché avendo mangiato

112. .... a casa, abbiamo fatto subito una doccia.
   a) avendo arrivati   b) arrivato
   c) arrivati   d) essendo arrivato

113. Ho un sonno terribile, ... vado a letto di corsa.
   a) ma   b) altrimenti
   c) perciò   d) tuttavia

114. Va' più piano, ... usciamo di strada.
   a) altrimenti   b) perciò
   c) quindi   d) ma

115. Sono mesi che non fumo, ... ho ancora voglia.
   a) anche   b) neanche
   c) altrimenti   d) tuttavia

116. In questa agenzia posso fare tutto, ... tradurre
   manuali tecnici.
   a) anche se   b) senza che
   c) tranne che   d) a meno che non

117. Oggi pomeriggio, ... piove, vado nei boschi.
   a) affinché   b) malgrado
   c) sebbene   d) anche se

118. .... non ti ho visto arrivare, sono partito.
   a) dal momento che   b) sebbene
   c) prima che   d) mentre

119. .... abbia già 30 anni, Mario ragiona ancora
   come un bambino.
   a) anche se   b) non appena
   c) dato che   d) sebbene

120. Bevi un caffè, ... tu possa riprenderti dopo questo test.
   a) cosicché   b) anche se
   c) poiché   d) che

Chiavi test di autovalutazione

1.	c)	32.	d)
2.	b)	33.	b)
3.	c)	34.	c)
4.	d)	35.	d)
5.	b)	36.	a)
6.	b)	37.	c)
7.	c)	38.	c)
8.	c)	39.	d)
9.	d)	40.	c)
10.	b)	41.	c)
11.	c)	42.	a)
12.	a)	43.	b)
13.	a)	44.	b)
14.	c)	45.	b)
15.	b)	46.	c)
16.	d)	47.	c)
17.	a)	48.	a)
18.	c)	49.	c)
19.	c)	50.	d)
20.	a)	51.	b)
21.	d)	52.	a)
22.	d)	53.	c)
23.	c)	54.	d)
24.	c)	55.	b)
25.	c)	56.	a)
26.	c)	57.	b)
27.	b)	58.	a)
28.	a)	59.	c)
29.	b)	60.	d)
30.	d)	61.	d)
31.	a)	62.	a)

63.	a)	95.	d)
64.	a)	96.	b)
65.	b)	97.	a)
66.	b)	98.	d)
67.	d)	99.	d)
68.	c)	100.	c)
69.	b)	101.	c)
70.	a)	102.	d)
71.	d)	103.	b)
72.	c)	104.	c)
73.	c)	105.	a)
74.	b)	106.	a)
75.	d)	107.	c)
76.	d)	108.	d)
77.	a)	109.	c)
78.	c)	110.	b)
79.	b)	111.	c)
80.	b)	112.	c)
81.	d)	113.	c)
82.	c)	114.	a)
83.	c)	115.	d)
84.	a)	116.	c)
85.	a)	117.	d)
86.	a)	118.	a)
87.	c)	119.	d)
88.	d)	120.	a)
89.	d)		
90.	c)		
91.	b)		
92.	b)		
93.	d)		
94.	b)		

Finito di stampare nel mese di novembre 2005
da Guerra guru s.r.l. - Via A. Manna, 25 - 06132 Perugia
Tel. +39 075 5289090 - Fax +39 075 5288244
E-mail: geinfo@guerra-edizioni.com